LIMITING OUT FOR CRAPPIE

Tim Huffman

LIMITING OUT FOR CRAPPIE
Copyright © 2018
All rights reserved.

No parts of this book may be reproduced in any form without permission.

ISBN# 978-0-9989089-0-8

Huffman Publishing

LIMITING OUT is written as a guide for fishing the four seasons using various tactics and techniques. Spring includes shallow-water methods and using stealth tactics to reach more fish. Summer chapters focus upon the fast-growing crankbait tactics used to catch open-water, suspended fish. Fall features specific structures where crappie hide, tactics for catching them and fishing the fall turnover. Winter discusses lake drawdown, shallow casting and mid-depth and deep stumps. Final chapters include cleaning, cooking and people who have been difference makers in the sport. Experts share insight and experience to tie everything together to create a complete guide for seasons, methods and presentations.

TABLE OF CONTENTS

CHAPTER 1
Spring Fishing, 1

CHAPTER 2
Spring: Shallow-Water Tactics, 7

CHAPTER 3
Spring: Shallow Ditches, Drops and Channels, 13

CHAPTER 4
Sneaky Push-Poling, 17

CHAPTER 5
Power Pole Fishing, 21

CHAPTER 6
Spring: Factors & Tips, 25

CHAPTER 7
Summer Fishing, 31

CHAPTER 8
Longpole Pulling…
Poles Off-Set On Sides, 35

CHAPTER 9
Longline Pulling…Poles Off the Back, 37

CHAPTER 10
Longline Pulling…Planer Boards, 43

CHAPTER 11
Pushing…Poles Off the Front, 49

CHAPTER 12
Pushing…Bulldozing, 53

CHAPTER 13
Longline Pulling...with Sinkers, 57

CHAPTER 14
Easy/Versatile Setup...with Sinkers, 61

CHAPTER 15
Party Barge...Pulling & Pushing, 65

CHAPTER 16
Economy Trolling...Pulling One or Two Poles, 69

CHAPTER 17
Casting Crankbaits, 73

CHAPTER 18
Crankbaiting Miscellaneous, 75

CHAPTER 19
Summer Tips: No Crankbaits, 81

CHAPTER 20
Fall, 85

CHAPTER 21
Naturally Stained Water, 89

CHAPTER 22
Texas-Style Fishing, 91

CHAPTER 23
Oxbows, 93

CHAPTER 24
Clear Water, 95

CHAPTER 25
Intersections, 97

CHAPTER 26
Fall Turnover, 103

CHAPTER 27
Seasonal Structure…Visible Wood Structure, 107

CHAPTER 28
Fall Factors & Tips, 111

CHAPTER 29
Winter, 115

CHAPTER 30
Shallow-Water Casting, 119

CHAPTER 31
Slow Trolling Mid-Depths & Deep Water, 123

CHAPTER 32
Lake Drawdown, 133

CHAPTER 33
Factors & Tips – Winter, 137

CHAPTER 34
Caring for Your Catch, 143

CHAPTER 35
Cleaning, 151

CHAPTER 36
Cooking, 159

CHAPTER 37
The "Difference Makers" in Crappie Fishing, 163

APPENDIX, 183

CHAPTER 1

Spring Fishing

Limiting Out!!

Spring is "Crappie Season" when all fishermen, including novices, can fill their stringers and livewells. Crappie are moving into predictable, shallow-water patterns. It's the easiest time of year for limiting out.

Terms to Know (Spring)

- **Staging Areas:** Places where fish hold during prespawn until water conditions are right to go into the beds. Staging areas, also called holding areas, are key spots to learn.
- **Prespawn:** A period of time before the spawn when fish are moving toward spawning areas and positioning themselves in staging areas.
- **Spawn:** A time of work for a male, buck crappie when they build a bed, recruit a female, fertilize eggs

and protect them until after hatching and the fry are ready to leave the nest.
- **Postspawn:** A rest period lasting approximately two weeks after the spawn when crappie are scattered, suspended and not wanting to eat.

Key Facts & Concepts (Spring)

- Migration is when crappie travel from one seasonal home to another. In the spring, it is from winter homes, along channels, to staging areas and finally to their spawning sites.
- Are crappie spawning when the dogwoods bloom? The famous old-timer saying is based upon experience. The dogwoods were in bloom when they caught shallow, spawning crappie. Air temperatures warm up enough for dogwoods to bloom, at the same time the water warms for spawning, so the statement is usually true. However, a fisherman misses most of the best spawn fishing if he waits until the dogwoods bloom.
- Spring is a time of great fishing but the bite can be tough when a strong cold front moves through. Shallow fish are bothered by a barometric pressure change more than deep fish are bothered. A crappie chaser can usually catch fish in the same places but the bite will be slow to very slow, so be patient.

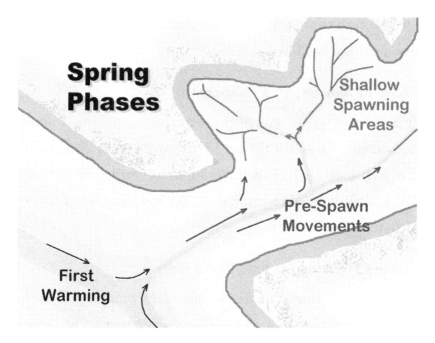

Spring Crappie Phases

Crappie migrate several times a year. Winter to spring movements reveal a pattern that every crappie fisherman should know. A look at various phases and timing patterns is a good way to understand the what, when and where of these movements.

Phase #1 Leaving Winter Homes

Crappie have been holding in open-water on deep ledges or other structure but now leave their winter homes. Movements are triggered by water temperatures, the amount of daylight, shad migrations or a combination of these and other factors. Fishermen and biologists sometimes differ on the specifics, but the results are the same as crappie graduate from deep water toward shallow.

Phase #2 Movements to Mid-Depths

In lakes with creek and river channels, crappie move along deep channels until they get to a favorite creek channel or bay. Channels are their primary highways for travel. In other lakes, it could be old weedlines, rocks, ledges or other cover/structure.

Phase #3 Making Shallow-Water Runs

While at the mouths of creeks and coves, crappie will likely make several runs into very shallow-water after a few days of good, warm weather. This shallow-water move is thought to be the start of the spawn by some fishermen, but the moves are actually feeding sprees that occur when the warming water draws baitfish. Late afternoons are usually the best fishing in the shallows because water is the warmest from the sun's rays. These shallow-water areas are typically at one extreme or the other, being dead or dynamite.

Phase #4 Staging for Spawn

Crappie move closer to spawning locations and hold in staging areas. Staging areas are places where they can feed yet move quickly into shallow-water. Or, if a terrible cold front hits, the crappie can slip back into deeper spots, usually the first drop-off. They'll stay in staging areas until conditions and temperatures are just right.

Phase #5 Spawning

Male crappie move into spawning areas to make beds. Once they have beds made and temperatures are correct, the females come in to lay eggs. Males fertilize the eggs and stay in to protect eggs and fry. Rising or falling water, rapidly changing temperatures and strong fronts are problems for the fish during this phase. But without a doubt, the survival of the eggs is dependent upon several factors including the male protecting them.

Phase #6 Postspawn

The post-spawn period will have a few late spawners still in shallower water. Female crappie finished with baby making will move out to nearby drops, creeks and flats. They will likely be suspended and lethargic, making them difficult to catch. The males soon follow. Within a week or two, the fish will start feeding.

Phase #7 Summer Homes

Crappie continue moving out to their summer homes although in some lakes the fish may stay shallow. Each lake and situation is different, so no blanket statements cover all lakes. However, in lakes where some of the fish stay up shallow for a longer period, the crappie are good targets, are often feeding and can be caught. Therefore, don't be in a big rush to move away from shallow-water.

Note: Spawning crappie are best known as shallow fish. However, many crappie never come into shallow-water. Be aware a percentage of fish may spawn in deeper water and in places you wouldn't expect. For example, in a big clear lake, the crappie may stay out and spawn on deep, rocky humps. Many lakes offer similar situations.

All 7 Phases of the Spawn

The above phases are guidelines. Crappie don't always follow the rules, so each lake and river can have different situations creating a variety of movement patterns. No matter what variations the fish may use, it's possible for you to learn their movements and learn what works on the waters you fish. Once a pattern of timing and places are learned, it's a good bet the ritual and pattern will be the same year after year.

CHAPTER 2
Spring: Shallow-Water Tactics

Dennis Bayles, Jr, calls Lake Conway, Arkansas, his home lake. He will fish several techniques but prefers single-pole jigging. His tactics on this trip can be applied to most shallow lakes or big lakes and rivers with shallow, stumpy coves and creek areas.

"In the winter, crappie are in the middle of the lake in the ponds. Fishing is great," Bayles says. "The fish start moving out of deep water in early March. The shallower crappie can create great fishing action."

The fish travel into shallow spots where fishermen have the opportunity to catch a big slab. Bayles says that shallow bays with three to five feet of water can be key areas when fish come in to spawn.

"It's late March," says Bayles, "and we are a little behind because of the cool winter. Fishing was excellent a few days ago, but a very strong front stopped the bite so it's tough right now. We are fishing shallow flats with a single-pole tightlining for crappie. We're looking for females coming into the shallow-water to spawn."

Visible and submerged stumps are key features, but we were moving along a little ledge. It was a big flat, but the stumps on the small drop were the best targets. Not believing that all crappie move to the shallowest water to spawn, Bayles prefers to target areas not pounded by other fishermen. He believes fishing pressure not only removes a percentage of the fish, but it makes them spooky and very difficult to catch. Those fish with less pressure are more likely to stay put and bite when a fisherman approaches.

"Travel isn't easy here on Lake Conway. The Game and Fish Commission has done a good job marking boat trails.

As long as you stay in the trails, you can travel just fine' but outside of the trails you need to shut off the big motor and use your trolling motor. Several of the boat-motor mechanics around the lake stay busy doing repairs due to the stumps doing damage."

His jigging tackle includes 11-foot Ozark rods, 6-pound Vicious line, MidSouth Super Jigs and 1/8-ounce heads, a lake map and an aluminum johnboat.

Another way Bayles catches crappie during prespawn conditions is by casting. When the water temperatures are in the mid 50s to lower 60s with fish three to five feet, they can be caught by casting. This is a good method when crappie are spooky and difficult to catch by tightlining. You can stay back from the fish and cast a jig under a float. Slow roll the jig back or bump the float occasionally, then let it rest.

Bayles prefers to use a 1/16-ounce jig under a light slip-float and use 4-pound-test line. Favorite colors includes a blue-white, black-white and black-clear on a bright day. On overcast days, he uses a black-chartreuse. Just recently his number-one pick is a white glitter with chartreuse. "There's something about the flash of the glitter that makes the bait look just like a baitfish. Just ask for the MidSouth Bayles color."

It's important when casting with a float and jig to set the hook hard. The reasons include the float causing an angle in the line that must be straightened, line stretch when using monofilament line and the bend of the pole. Therefore, the hard hookset quickly gets a fisherman in direct contact with the fish so the hook penetrates. It's light line, so a balance between good hookset and not breaking the line is critical. Once hooked up, a mild pressure is all that's needed to bring the fish to the boat. Experience teaches how much pressure is too little and how much pressure is too much. And sometimes, the fish wins even when a fisherman does everything correctly.

Spring spawn time can be great fishing, but you must find the fish and have cooperation from the weather. On my trip with Bayles, we caught only four or five fish on our afternoon of fishing although two crappie pushed two pounds and we lost a big fish. The next day he caught no fish. Day three he caught four. The fourth day following the front, and just before another front, he caught 40 fish, culling everything less than a pound. This goes along with the theory that fishing is tough following a front and continues to get better each day afterward. Bad days and good days are part of fishing. He has promised to take me on a great fishing trip to get in on the spring action this year.

Spring Tip: Spring crappie will spawn in correlation with water temperatures. Minnows are good bait this time of year. A double-hook Capps/Coleman-style minnow rig with a light 1/4-ounce egg sinker is good for fishing shallow-water. If fish go really shallow and into cover like pad stems, a

1/8-ounce single jig tipped with a small minnow is best for slow trolling. Colors vary, but a bright orange-chartreuse in muddy-stained water is good. In clearer waters, try a blue-white or blue-clear.

NOTES

CHAPTER 3

Spring: Shallow Ditches, Drops and Channels

What is shallow? The term "shallow" may mean two feet in some waters and eight feet in others, so different water conditions, including temperature and light penetration, are key factors to where you'll find crappie. No matter the depth, crappie prefer to be on a quick contour if one is in the area. A slope or drop offers many advantages that fish need.

Finding Fish. Locating shallow crappie hangouts can be difficult. A great way to find top spots is to scout the lake during low water conditions or drawdowns. All of the small drops can be seen and marked on your map. You can come back when water is normal and fish them.

Another scouting tool is Google Earth maps. Looking at a map during low water conditions can reveal cover, small ditches and other structures normally not seen. Expert fishermen are using these maps to do pre-trip scouting and planning.

GPS allows marking spots with waypoints. A fisherman can return to these locations quickly and easily.

A graph, also generically called sonar, locator or depth-finder, is a key tool for seeing fish but also for watching bottom depth. A fisherman can be fishing lily pads or stumps in three feet of water. The locator shows a sudden change from three feet to four feet. This is a small change that the average weekend fisherman may not notice. However, that quick change in the middle of an otherwise relatively flat area can be a goldmine for fish. Therefore, the moral is to pay attention for subtle depth changes that could point to a fantastic structure within an otherwise similar-looking area. Paying attention to small details is a critical link to better fishing. The locator is a tool to make it happen.

Final Notes. The previous segments are shallow-water fishing tactics for spring. The same tactics can be used any time the fish are in shallow-water. Every expert believes vertical jigging is a top pick in shallow, stump-filled water. The up and down presentation gives fewer hang-ups and lets you put the bait on the crappie's head. No other technique is more efficient in thick cover. In areas with less cover, slow trolling and casting can be good choices.

Sometimes flipping or casting lets you reach shallow openings and wood cover you can't reach with straight jigging. The flipped bait will often be hit on the fall. The pendulum motion back toward the fisherman gives an enticing presentation. Crappie have a difficult time ignoring a swinging, falling, natural-looking bait.

Some areas allow casting. When targeting bedding fish, a cast lets a fisherman stay a distance from the fish yet drop the bait right into their hangout. There's no crappie fishing more fun than casting to active, spawning male crappie. And crappie fishing should be about having fun. Top casting baits include a Road Runner, plain jig, jig/slip-float combo and minnow/slip-float.

NOTES

CHAPTER 4
Sneaky Push-Poling

Here's one tactic that any fishing-boat owner can afford to do. It doesn't require an expensive trolling motor or high-dollar locator electronics. Although a few may curl their noses at the technique, it has proven its value at catching crappie. It takes work, patience and quiet, but I give it a big thumbs-up for stalking spooky, shallow-water crappie.

Mike Walters is an accomplished tournament fisherman with many great finishes. He and his son took third in the 2013 Crappie Masters Classic. He is still making classics, including the 2017 fall classics. He is from Ohio but is excellent on southern lakes, too, especially Grenada.

Walter's strong suit is versatility. Tournament fishing forces a fisherman to adapt to conditions, situations and therefore techniques. He has learned how to fish many different ways so he can adapt to any conditions he faces and still be successful. One tactic he has used in special, super-shallow situations is push-pole fishing.

Walters says, "We use the poles to push us along in shallow-water, usually in water too shallow for the trolling motor. We use the poles to quietly move us and to anchor. We simply get to where we want to fish, push them into the mud, tie a rope to them and then tie to the boat. It keeps the boat still."

The equipment is simple and inexpensive. The pole is 10-foot, 2-inch PVC pipe with a T-handle on one end.

"Rick Solomon and I won a tournament in the fall using these, but they are really good in the spring. We use them when tournament fishing and when fishing for fun. Actually, any time when the fish are in shallow-water. We use the trolling motor if we have to, but the key is to leave it turned off and push until we get within flipping range," says Walters. "We don't want too close because it's so shallow. Sometimes we'll add a tiny float for a strike indicator so we can cast. We work it the same as we would any other jigging technique."

Being quiet is critical. One trick is to let the wind move the float up against cover. When fish are tight, it's a deadly trick.

Walters says to work areas slowly and methodically. Without a float, slowly drop a jig down beside a stump. Slowly lift it up. Maintain contact with the jig, and place the line in your fingers while letting the rod blank rest in your fingers because it increases your sensitivity.

When using a float, cast up-wind, let it blow the float against the stump and let it stay there. Take it away slowly, jiggle and stop. Any movement at all means it's time to set the hook. The trick is to cast to tight spots and keep it beside the wood for a while.

Walters and his partner use two push poles to move the boat along in the shallow-water. They quietly position the boat in the location they want and then shove each pole into the mud with one near the front and one near the back of the boat. They tie the poles to the boat. When finished, they use one snap-pull to remove each pole from the mud.

Equipment includes a BnM 12-foot jigging pole, 1/16-ounce Southern Pro jig and 8-pound-test line.

Note: In today's world, the push poles get little notice because of fishermen being in the habit of using trolling motors. Power poles are good shallow power anchors with many high-dollar boats rigging with them, reducing the need for push poles. However, Solomon and Walters say the push-pole tactics are still as good in 2018 as they were twenty years ago.

Spring Tip: Begin your spring search for crappie at the mouth of a creek. Work toward the back. The crappie will be somewhere in the creek and will usually be along gradient lines you'll find on the map. Trust your electronics to help you find the fish and to see how they are positioned. Learn the right depths and you'll find fish in similar areas.

CHAPTER 5
Power Pole Fishing

Power Anchors: there's no easier way stabilize a boat in shallow water. A push of a switch moves the pole downward into the lake bottom to anchor the boat.

Charles and Travis Bunting won the American Crappie Trail 2017 Classic Championship. They've also won the Crappie USA National Points Title, Crappie Masters 2009 Mississippi State Championship and the 2012 Crappie Masters National Championship. The father/son fishing team lives in Missouri and calls Lake of the Ozarks and Truman Lake home waters.

Charles Bunting says, "The Power Pole holds you dead still in the wind. Depending upon the model, our first ones had eight feet of adjustment so basically, when we were in seven feet or less, we could drop it down and it held us still in a 50-mile-per-hour wind. It's hydraulic operated and can be controlled from a switch on the front or from a remote control. On a glass boat, the pole is mounted to a plate that goes between the jack plate and boat. On an aluminum boat there is a plate.

"You can use it in any shallow water on any lake," continues Charles. "We use the poles all the time when fishing waters like Conway and Reelfoot Lakes. We also use it in shallow water a lot at Truman. We like to head to where we want to fish, let off the trolling motor and glide into the spot. We put down the poles so we have a very quiet approach. After dropping the poles, we can fish quietly from an anchored boat. It's great."

"I love the poles," says Travis Bunting. "It's changed our fishing because it allows us to fish shallow water more consistently. Using them makes the fish less spooky, so we catch more. For example, at Conway, Arkansas, we fished a lot of six-foot water. We would go with the wind, and when we would get to where we wanted to fish, we would just drop the Power Poles to stop us. We didn't need to have our trolling motor running."

Shallow water is not the only use for the Power Poles. The pole can be used to raise a chain up and down when dragging it to slow the boat in the wind. It can also be used to lift a drift sock up and down without leaving your seat. Travis says, "Even when fishing a slick bottom, you have to be adjusting chain depths so the Power Poles really help. Also, when the chain gets hung, we just lift the Power Pole and it breaks the chain free. We can drop it back down. We still use the chains but Drift Paddles attached to the poles is another way to control the boat speed and angle of drift. They let us have control in deeper water without moving from our seats."

Spring Tip: Spring fishing can be tough with a wide variety of conditions presenting problems. High water is one situation. It can be difficult, but after you have it figured out, you will catch a bunch of fish. High water means there are big storms that have moved through bringing rains. When water is rising, the best choice is usually going to cleaner water in the lower part of the lake. After a few days, it's best to go way upriver and into creeks because the backs of those are the first to start clearing up.

NOTES

CHAPTER 6
Spring: Factors & Tips

Wind: Spring is famous for wind, or more correctly, infamous. It can make boat positioning a challenge or impossible. It bounces baits up and down, reducing the number of bites. The wind also causes a fisherman to take a beating when crossing open-water.

Water Color: Stained water makes vertical fishing much easier. The approach is less critical. Clear water has spooky crappie that forces a fisherman to adjust methods. For example, shallow, clear-water crappie may require casting instead of jigging.

Cold Front: Spring is known for strong cold fronts. These fronts are frequent, with the general rule-of-thumb being good fishing right before and during the front followed by worse fishing after it passes. It's all about the barometric pressure changes. Therefore, clear, bluebird skies following a front is typically tough fishing in the spring or any other season.

Blakemore Roadrunner & Charlie Brewer Crappie Slider Grub

Fishing Pressure: Everyone has cabin fever, they know that spring is a good time to catch crappie, so fishing pressure is heavy in the spring. Fishing pressure means crowded ramps and usually too many fishermen in the good areas of the lake. But, everyone loves to fish, so a fisherman has to be mentally prepared to handle the fact that other fishermen will be there, too.

Air Temperature: A few days of warm weather can trigger great action. The opposite is true when you get a few days of cold temperatures. Cooling water makes fish very negative. Pay attention because fishing speed and what a fisherman should expect are closely related to fish aggressiveness. When fish are negative, it's time to go super-slow.

Question: Jigheads with blades are popular. When do crappie want a blade and how do you select the best size and color?

Mr. Crappie, Wally Marshall, says, "For 25 years I've used a blade for crappie. I fish a lot of murky water, and the blade vibration gives more bites even when vertical jigging. It helps me catch a lot more fish.

"I seldom use a blade when finesse fishing, like shooting docks. That's when I switch to a Slab Daddy jig. Also, when fishing any technique, there are times when crappie want a blade and times they don't, like when they are in their deep winter homes. Blades are great for catching crappie, but there are times when they work and times they don't. It's like loving a steak, but there are times we prefer biscuits and gravy. Same with a crappie."

"Gold or silver? I use the Road Runner Pro Series with the gold blade because it produces fish. I use the 1/8-ounce head when vertical jigging because it keeps me in better contact with the jig. In bushes and trees, it gives a better feel. A bigger hook is another advantage. A 1/16-ounce is better for casting because it has a slower fall."

Jim Reedy, a tournament fisherman who lives in Missouri, says, "I use Road Runners. The blades usually work better in stained or muddy water because they add a little flash and attraction. I prefer the Pro Series Road Runners with the willow-leaf blades. They are a little longer and they seem to work better in stained water. I also like the silver because they seem to work in waters with good light penetration. So when the water is a little clearer or the crappie are up higher in the water, the silver gets a good flash and the crappie like that."

Travis Bunting, says, "A blade is really good during the pre-spawn and for pitching to the banks. It's also good when the fish move back out and we push or troll. We'll use a blade all year except in the winter when the fish want a smaller bait and less flash.

"We'll use them all summer jigging. We prefer using a big #3 blade. In clear water we use a silver blade. We use a Pro Series Road Runner with a gold willow leaf blade when visibility is less than a foot and a half."

Jim Duckworth, a Tennessee guide, has a good tip. "I'm a Road Runner guy. I paint one or both sides of a blade to get the color I want for the water being fished. Paint them before heading to the lake or carry a variety of Magic Markers, like a yellow, red, green and black, to make changes while fishing. Sometimes a little color change will make a lot of difference. For years I've paid close attention to the colors and it's true with all species including crappie."

More Spring Tips

Bruce Christian from southeast Missouri is an avid recreational fisherman and tournament fisherman. He and his partner finished 14 out of 124 boats in the 2017 Crappie Masters National Championship.

May crappie are postspawn in his regional waters. "My tip would be to move fast. The crappie move out away from structure and suspend up in the water. We pull for them as fast as 1.5 mph with crankbaits and at 0.8 mph with jigs. A fisherman needs to cover a lot of water because the crappie aren't real active, so baits need to be put in front of a lot of fish. Any type of twister-tail bait will usually work because they have action. Southern Pro and Bobby Garland are two popular ones. Use one 1/16-ounce head when fish are up high and switch to two 1/16-ounce jigs when fish are down some. We pull jigs at 0.5 to 0.8 mph.

"One other tip is to try a Road Runner head. It's one of those things you have to try to see if it works. Sometimes the fish really like it and other times they won't hit it."

Jim Dant says he catches fish in the pads at Reelfoot Lake all the way up until July when hot weather hits. "I single-pole fish in the pads using a BnM Sam Heaton 11-foot jigging pole. I use two poles with two different jigs. That means two colors. I like Bobby Garland in natural shade colors, silver flake and gold flake. Lights Out, a black-chartreuse glow, is another good color. My best pad tip is to start at the top and work down. A lot of times the black crappie are right under the pads. Then I go all the way down to the bottom and pick it up six inches. That's where the white crappie usually are located."

Find visible cover. "I'll be jig fishing," says Wally Marshall. "I'll use a 10-foot rod. What I'm looking for is visible cover because what crappie will do in the springtime is get up in the shallows. They'll be 2 to 6 feet deep on stumps, laydowns, logs and any structure sticking up above the surface. It's difficult to use electronics to find cover not sticking up because of the shallow depths. Vegetation is good, too, because it provides protection and shade."

A good presentation. Marshall says, "For our example, we'll consider a stumpfield. The stumps will have root systems you can't see with the naked eye. So, when running the jig around, it's good to bring it out from the stump for maybe five feet. Keep the jig swimming or walking the dog around the roots. Other stumps you find that you can't see are a bonus. My jig will be a Strike King, maybe a Sausagehead jig with plastic in hotchicken.com color, bright pink and vibrant chartreuse tail."

River Fishing Tip: Points can be good when water is being pulled. Fish stack up on the backside of points. They'll be out of the current waiting for baitfish to come to them. The big ones like to be lazy and wait for food instead of exerting energy. The key for catching will be using the right technique to fish the point based upon its size, how fish relate to cover and the mood of the fish.

CHAPTER 7
Summer Fishing

Limiting Out!!

Catching a crappie in the summer isn't as difficult as many people think. However, catching a limit of really big fish is a huge challenge. On many lakes, trolling crankbaits gives you the best chance of catching big slabs and limiting out.

Terms to Know (Summer)
- Thermocline: A thin, horizontal layer separating water with good oxygen from bad water with low oxygen. Active crappie will be in good water above the thermocline. The thermocline can be seen on a locator with sensitivity turned up.
- Suspended, Scattered Crappie: Fish that are randomly positioned; opposite of being tight to cover at a specific depth. Fast techniques are usually required because fish are scattered.

- Crankbait: A hard, artificial bait that imitates a baitfish. There are no limits to shapes and sizes. The popular ones for crappie are in the 2- to 2.75-inch range. Most include a large lip so they will go deep. Crappie prefer one crankbait over another, but it's impossible to predict which one it will be on a particular day. The standard for crappie is the Bandit 300-series crank, but several others are used, too.
- Planer Board: A gadget with clips, and sometimes a flag, that connects to the line and takes the bait away from the boat. It provides more line separation, a wider trolling path and gets baits away from the boat. When crappie are a little spooky, nothing beats planer boards. Off-Shore has a smaller model marketed in 2017 specifically for pulling crankbaits and jigs for crappie and similar sized fish.
- Pulling: A technique where baits are trolled behind the boat. Baits are pulled.
- Pushing: A technique where baits are fished out the front of the boat. Baits are ahead of the motor and trolling motor so therefore are being pushed.

Key Facts and Concepts (Summer)
- Crankbait technique systems are expensive.
- Big deep flats are good places to crankbait. So are creek and river channels.

- Keep all lines and baits the same size and brand for consistency.
- Crankbaiting is an excellent method in the wind.

Guide to Summer Crankbait Crappie

"Where do the big ones go in the summer?" That's a big problem. Smaller fish can be caught, but the big slabs seem to disappear during the mid-summer heat.

I read a study several years ago where three identical ponds were stocked with all sizes of crappie. One pond was left natural, another had baitfish introduced periodically, and the third one had an aerator unit to cool and oxygenate the water. It was a summertime study.

In pond number one, the pond that was left natural, the crappie had little growth, especially big crappie. Only small crappie could be caught. Pond number two had baitfish introduced throughout the study; smaller fish had moderate growth but larger fish did not grow. Again, only the small fish could be caught. Pond number three with aeration had growth of all crappie sizes, and all size fish could be caught.

The theory was formed that big slab crappie become somewhat dormant during the heat of summer due to hot water and less oxygen. They will eat but usually just to sustain life. It's basically heat stress. It bothers the older, large crappie much more than the young ones. Therefore, big crappie can be difficult to catch in summer.

Crankbait fishermen have theories, too. Fishermen have learned that the big crappie from postspawn through fall will usually suspend in open water. They are difficult to catch using typical methods. Pulling crankbaits is different because a lot of baits are presented to many fish. Some crappie may see the bait and then strike due to hunger, but the bites are more likely reaction strikes. Fish hear the bait coming, see it and have a short period of time to hit it or let it go, so they strike it. Crankbaits can be pulled along big flats, over channels and other mid-depth or deep-water areas to catch fish.

Tip: Non-crankbait tactics work, too. For success with slower presentations, it's important to locate schools of fish. Odds improve if crappie are around cover and baitfish are present.

Slow trolling can be a good technique. Homework should be done with the electronics to ensure the area has good potential.

You'll hear people say the summertime fish don't bite, but that's not true. They are just more finicky. The fast trollers get reaction bites, but slow trolling is a feeding bite, so small baits are good. Downsize to 6-pound-test line and smaller jigs and minnows. A small minnow on the back of the right-colored jig will catch fish. Go slower.

CHAPTER 8

Longpole Pulling...
Poles Off-Set On Sides

Setup Note: This technique is only moderately difficult to learn and perform. Basic setup costs are moderate to expensive. Effectiveness rating: 9 out of 10.

Equipment List
- Almost any boat.
- Line-counter reels.
- Racks/holders with strong holders on the sides.
- Trolling poles 16-, 12- and 8-foot lengths.

Setup

Proper setup for crankbaits depends upon the number of poles you use. Two on each side isn't difficult, and by using 12- and 16-foot poles, you can get good separation with fewer tangles plus you keep the baits a distance away from the boat. A three-poles-per-side setup uses 8-, 12- and 16-foot poles.

Four poles per side require a 10-foot pole between the 8 and 12. However, four feet separation is best for all but experienced, expert pullers.

Fishing

Place a crankbait into the water and free-spool it back until it reaches the right distance. The simplest way to keep things in order is to always have the outside pole out the longest distance back. A sample setup is 200 feet for the outside pole, 150 feet for the middle pole and 100 feet for the inside pole.

When a fish is caught, work it between other poles. There will still be some tangles, but they'll be kept to a minimum. When the strike zone is found, you can make other poles closer to the same depth, but always keep some pole-length difference to help reduce tangles.

This system offers a wide trolling path, a moderate turning radius and allows different depths to be fished simultaneously. The staggered pole system makes sense.

Tips & Tricks

- By aligning the poles properly with the longest in front and shortest in back, you can get the pole tips to line up in a straight line at a 90-degree angle in reference to the side of the boat. This is great because you'll quickly see when one is out of line. Bites, fouled crankbaits or any other changes will be easier to see.

CHAPTER 9

Longline Pulling... Poles Off the Back

Setup Note: This technique is moderately difficult to learn, moderate to perform, has moderate setup costs. Effectiveness rating: 7 out of 10.

Brad Whitehead is a fishing guide in northern Alabama. He is at home on many of the north and northwest Alabama waters and Mississippi lakes. He isn't afraid to do something different to match a tactic to what the fish are doing. His favorite technique is side-pulling jigs, but he will pull crankbaits much of the summer. I've had the opportunity to share the boat with him several times.

Equipment List

- 754 War Eagle boat.
- Happy Troller plate and big motor.
- BnM 8-foot Difference rods; along with longer Pro Staff poles.
- Spinning reels with Vicious 10-pound test line.

Setup

Brad's tiller boat gives him more room than with a console boat. He fishes either four or six poles out the back. If he wants more poles, he adds 10, 12 and 14 footers out the side. The trolling plate on his motor helps maintain the right trolling speed.

Getting ready to fish is easy because everything is out the back. He finds his location, starts his run and sets his baits.

"I troll forward," says Whitehead. "I like using the big motor, so I don't have to fool with charging batteries all the time. And with a four-stroke motor it's fuel efficient and quiet."

"I like to set my lines to different lengths until I learn which line length the fish are holding. When I catch a couple of fish at one length, I'll mark the line with a number-two Magic Marker so I don't have to count line pulls; just let line out to the mark on the line.

"Getting the length right is critical. I count out line on my poles by letting out six feet of line at a time. You can do the same thing by putting a piece of white tape at a six-foot mark from the reel. Counting by six-foot pulls is more accurate than two- or three-foot pulls."

He says many different brands of crankbaits will get the job done. He has successfully used Lindy Shadlings, Bandits and others.

Fishing

Whitehead's fishing while pulling is straight and simple. Poles out the back and watching for a bite. "My favorite crankbait time is late summer and early fall. I'm typically fishing in medium to deep water. Find a good area and it will likely stay good for a while. If fish move, it will probably be a little deeper or shallower. They don't make a big move.

"Crappie suspend in deeper water, making them perfect for crankbaits. However, you have to get the baits to them because they won't go far up or down to get one."

He says a typical spot is an 18-foot-deep area that's 100 yards from a 30-feet-deep channel. The fish will likely be somewhere near the creek or river channel.

"A crankbait is different in that fishing often gets better up in the middle of the day when it's hottest. Where I fish as the fall temperatures cool the water, the fish will migrate out toward the channel for a while, but then they'll get out and start chasing balls of shad and might go anywhere."

Bonus Poles

Although Whitehead likes to keep it simple, for the past couple of years while pulling the cranks, he adds two or four 16-foot poles out the front during tough-to-catch conditions. He puts a 5-ounce sinker on the end of the line. Up 18 inches in front of the sinker is a 1/8-ounce jig. Another jig is added 18 inches above the first jig.

"I prefer to pull just the crankbaits, but there is no need being hard headed when fishing is tough and I can catch more fish by adding the bonus poles. It has paid off big-time."

Tips & Tricks

- Make fishing more fun and less work with a good, simple setup. Too much work reduces the enjoyment of the sport.
- No matter the trolling technique used, Whitehead will put buoys out in big areas where he is fishing. "I'll put three buoys about 300 yards apart and in fun I'll call it the "triangle of death". Even though I have mapping and GPS, it just makes it easier to have visual locators."

Tip: No matter the season, no matter the technique, one thing stays constant…don't keep doing what isn't working.

So if a fisherman is fast trolling with cranks and fish aren't biting, it's time to change depth, speeds and bait colors. Keep trying combinations until the crappie show what they want. After dialing into a specific pattern, catching more fish in different areas of the lake is possible.

Slow trollers also should change up when not catching fish. Vary depths in areas where fish are known to be located. It's okay to go shallow when fish won't hit deep, and to go deeper. Tip jigs with minnows. Try minnows by themselves. Slow down and speed up. A key to catching fish is to find active fish, and give them what they want, the way they want it. Don't keep doing what isn't working!

NOTES

CHAPTER 10
Longline Pulling...Planer Boards

Setup Note: This technique is difficult to learn, moderately difficult and awkward to perform, basic setup cost moderate to high, with advanced setup very expensive. Effectiveness rating: 10 out of 10.

Stan Tallant is a Mississippi fisherman who spends time on the water at Sardis, Arklabutla and Grenada lakes. His primary waters in Mississippi are some of the best in the country for pulling crankbaits.

Planer board fishing is a method not often seen in the South until recent years. A Crappie Masters Classic win at Grenada, Mississippi a few years ago by a walleye expert brought attention to the tactic for crappie.

Tallant's theory is that crappie are spooked by boat pressure and motor noise. The fish move to the side of the boat. Planer boards reach both the crappie that are positioned away from the boat, along with the fish that are spooked and move off to the side to get out of the way. When the bait comes by about 15 seconds later, they instinctively hit it.

Learning the technical aspects of the method isn't too difficult, but it requires some practice to get all the steps right. It's awkward removing a planer board when you have a big fish on.

Equipment List

- Minn Kota Terrova for automatic steering and remote control.
- Off-Shore planer boards with flag kits.
- Driftmaster rack and Driftmaster Little Duo holders.
- Bass Pro Shops Tourney Special 7-foot medium-heavy poles.
- Okuma model 20 line-counter reels.
- 10-pound high-visibility P-Line
- Primary baits are 300-series Bandits; others include 200-series Bandit, Yo-zuri, Mann's 15+ and Rapala JSR5.
- Special rig consisting of a snap-on 1-ounce weight to get baits deeper.

Setup

Tallant gets his boat into position, sets the autopilot trolling motor and puts poles out. "We always introduce baits to the back of the boat. The planer boards will go where they need

to go and get out of the way of the next bait to be introduced. When four planer boards are used out the back, the planer board distance from the boat is 50 and 100 feet or 60 and 40. Four boards are good when fish are only hitting the outside plugs. When fishing one board per side, use a 60-foot board distance. I prefer to catch fish as close to the boat as possible."

Here are the steps. One, introduce the bait to the back of the boat and let it freespool to the distance you want. Remember that it takes less line from a planer board at water level compared to poles sticking up high in the air. Two, clip the planer board onto the line when you have the amount of line you want the bait running. Step three, let the planer board out whatever distance from the boat you want. Four, place pole in holder.

Fishing

The key to Tallant's technique is the Terrova trolling motor (any auto-control model will work). Once set, the motor stays on course without further attention. When it is time to turn or change speeds, Tallant does it from a wristwatch-style controller. He can stay at the back of the boat and control the motor. He says that nothing is worse than a motor without automatic control because anything from catching a fish to changing baits can be disaster when the boat spins with lines out.

Trolling speed is typically 1.7 miles per hour. Areas can be anything from creeks to flats depending upon where the fish are located. Since the tactic allows a lot of water to be covered, it is possible to cover several types of bottom contours in a short period.

"I have a flag on the planer board and use the reel's clicker system to indicate bites. With crappie you have to have the flag or you can't see when you have a fish.

"When I get a hit on the outside pole, I'm going to release the inside pole and let it go back while I pull the fish in. The pole that was on the inside will then become the outside pole. After the catch, I'll release the spool on the pole that just caught the fish and place the bait in the water in back of the boat."

Tallant says putting the planer board on the line is fairly simple. He places the line into the clip and closes it. He then makes a wrap around the clip and runs it through the clip again. This holds the line, yet the line will pop out immediately when he releases the clip. Pull about 10 inches of slack line and attach it to the flag. Check to make sure the flag works easily and then drop the planer board into the water.

Removing the board is easier with two people but can be done when fishing alone. Reel the line until you get to the planer board. Remove the planer board, release the line without popping it, and reel the fish into the boat or net.

Tips & Tricks

- Catch fish with a kicker minnow. Tie the hook 20 to 30 inches above the crankbait. "I think it's something else to draw their attention," says Tallant. "Sometimes I catch a lot on the minnows."
- While Tallant and I were fishing at Sardis, the fish were hitting better by pulling jigs at a slower speed, a different technique than crankbaits. While trolling the jigs, he experimented by using a long kicker pole with a crankbait on it. We learned that fish would hit the crankbait while trolling at 0.9 mph. After catching a few quality fish, we switched everything to crankbaits and started catching more fish at the slow speed.
- Have a cheat sheet somewhere easy to see so you can set your baits to the exact depth you want the bait

to go. Tallant created his from the book, Precision Trolling. A laminated cheat sheet on a trolling rack makes a great reference. Today there is a phone app to make it easy.

Summer Tip: Every day is different. Sometimes they slam a bait, and sometimes they just mess around with it. The biggest thing in summer fishing is developing a pattern. If you go to the lake forcing the crappie to take trolled crankbaits on a big flat, you are limiting yourself. You need to find what the fish are doing, where they are doing it and adjust to them. No matter the season, finding a pattern is a critical element of crappie fishing.

CHAPTER 11
Pushing…Poles Off the Front

Setup Note: This technique is moderately difficult to learn, extremely difficult to perform, moderate to expensive for basic setup and very expensive for advanced setup. Effectiveness rating: 8 out of 10.

Equipment List
- Any type boat but a big front deck is an advantage.
- Very strong, racks and holders in front.
- Stiff, strong 16-foot poles; example, BnM Pro Staff or Pow-R-Troller
- Heavy baitcaster reels.
- 17- to 20-pound-test line.
- Crankbait
- 5-ounce egg sinkers.

Pushing off of the front of the boat can be dangerous because of the long poles, flopping fish, crankbait treble hooks and a big sinker swinging around. It's not simple and not for someone weak. It requires a lot of work. On the positive side, it makes depth control easy. Boat control is the best possible and allows you to follow contours or any other structure feature.

Setup

Setting up requires finding your area, placing baits in the water and poles in holders. It's much simpler to place and set depths compared to pulling.

The primary rigging is Carolina style and includes the main line, an egg sinker, bead and swivel, five-foot leader to a snap swivel and bait. Some fishermen prefer to use a three-way swivel and leader going to a river type or bell sinker instead of having the weight inline.

Fishing

Take the baits anywhere you want. You need to stay in relatively deep or mid-depth waters, but you can troll flats, channels and points because the boat is very easy to control. The poles are in front of you, making it simple to change depths if contours change.

The difficult part is handling the poles. Just getting a pole out of the rack requires strength. It's not easy to use a 16-foot pole to swing a big sinker and big crappie to the top of the water and keep it under control. Most fish are brought in by swinging them into the boat using the rod holder as an anchor point. Crankbaits are a pain to get loose from the net every time. But even when netting, there is still a big sinker swinging around with treble hooks looking to find something to grab.

NOTES

CHAPTER 12
Pushing...Bulldozing

Setup Note: Moderately difficult to learn, extremely difficult to perform, has moderate to expensive setup costs. Effectiveness rating: 9 out of 10.

Equipment List

Ronnie Capps and Steve Coleman are known as one of the best crappie fishing teams in the country. In 2013 they won their eighth national championship, taking the Crappie USA Classic at Kentucky Lake. In 2017, they won the American Crappie Trail Angler of the Year Championship, finished 8th in the ACT National Championship and 10th in the Crappie USA Classic.

The team is known for their slow-trolling expertise. However, they'll change gears when necessary and push crankbaits.

The Capps/Coleman checklist
- Large glass boat.
- Tite-Lok single-pole holders.

- BnM 16-foot Pro Staff poles and spinning reels.
- 25-pound P-Line.
- Bandit baits.
- 4-, 5- and 6-ounce sinkers

Bulldozing

Unlike most fishermen, the team uses two crankbaits per pole. "You need a hard hat and any other protection you can get," says Capps. "It's a meat-in-the-pot technique that lets you wear them out when they're hitting. It's no sport, not fun and more like combining a field during harvest except we're doing it in water for fish."

The team uses BnM Pro Staff Trolling Poles with BnM reels but admit they go through a lot of reels because they treat them so rough. They use 25-pound-test P-Line.

"The tactic has advantages," says Coleman. "the biggest being the amount of water that can be covered. Also, the baits can usually be ripped through the cover. Another advantage is you'll find cover you wouldn't with other methods, and then come back later to fish it with a slow technique."

"Our rig starts with a sinker on bottom," says Capps. "Our sinker is 4-, 5- or 6-ounce. Up two inches to a three-way swivel, a 30-inch dropper and what we call a 300-series Bandit digger. The bait gets below the sinker when running and really digs in. Up about 36 inches, we have another three-way swivel, a 30-inch leader and a 100- or 200-series shallower bait. We're pushing and covering about a 50-inch vertical span of water. Most of the time we can rip the rig out of cover when it hangs. The lip is usually what hangs anyway."

The team says that a lot of hits come when the bait contacts cover or when they rip it loose from the cover when it hangs. The line strength allows them to get free without breaking off, and the bigger line size doesn't matter with this method.

The team says a double-crankbait setup along with a sinker and flopping fish can be very dangerous and recommend that beginners always learn using one bait per pole.

Capps says, "Concerning crankbaits, there are a lot of different baits that catch crappie. We've switched and swapped and at the end of the day seem to always have Bandits on because they catch more fish."

Tip: Summer trolling is great for finding and catching crappie, but it has another huge advantage. Paying attention to the graph allows a fisherman to find and mark spots he would never find when slow fishing. These marked spots can be fished later and during other seasons with slow presentation methods. Scouting is an important part of fishing, and fast trolling allows scouting and fishing to be done simultaneously.

NOTES

CHAPTER 13
Longline Pulling...with Sinkers

Setup Note: This technique is easy-moderate to learn and perform, the basic setup cost can be low to moderate. Effectiveness rating: 4 out of 10.

Equipment List
- Any style boat.
- Simple or advanced electronics.
- Trolling plate on big motor, kicker motor or autopilot-style trolling motor.
- Best with staggered 8-, 12- and 16-foot poles.
- Line-counter reels okay but not required when using sinkers.
- Sinkers are 2- to 4-ounce.
- A 2-ounce sinker rig on the main line followed by bead and a swivel. From the other side of the swivel, tie a 5-foot leader with a snap swivel on the end. Attach a crankbait to the snap swivel.

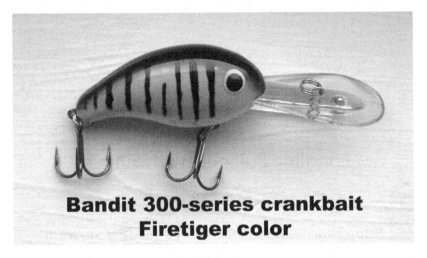

Bandit 300-series crankbait Firetiger color

Sinkers are very different in presentation but have several distinct advantages. One, depth is easier to control because less line is used. Two, turning can be much quicker because you don't have line 200 feet behind the boat. Three, if you stop your boat, the baits just settle down instead of rising.

Setup

The setup depends upon the type poles and sinker size. You can vary your sinker size with the lightest one in back and the heaviest in front. For example, use a 1-ounce in back, then 2-ounce and so on toward the front. Or, the simplest and preferred method is to vary the pole lengths and use the same sinker weight, usually a 2-ounce egg sinker. Whatever you use, test different options to see what works best for you.

Rig properly. Inline sinkers are good but need to have a bead and swivel below them to reduce the chance of weakening the line. The swivel helps avoid line twists.

Fishing

Find the right spot. As previously mentioned, a big flat is always a good starting point with cranks but because there is better control of the baits with this method, a fisherman may choose to fish a channel. Controlling speed is similar to the other methods with 1.5 to 2.0 miles per hour being a good range most of the time.

Sinker size determines vertical depth and how much line will be out. For example, if you use 2-ounce sinkers, your line angle will be moderate. However, the amount of line required is minimal compared to longlining with no weight. You'll soon learn how to best measure your line and set baits at an exact depth.

The major downside to this tactic is that fish often prefer baits to be further away from the boat. When fish are finicky, it is not the best tactic for catching fish.

Tips & Tricks

- Pick the size sinker to use, put the bait out on 30 feet of line, the boat speed at 1.5 mph and slowly work toward shallower water. When the bait starts bumping bottom, check the locator for water depth. Let out different line lengths to learn bait-and-sinker combos and their depth. Write down the results to make a "cheat sheet" reference.

- Never forget that using sinkers adds a slight danger when hoisting in a fish on a long pole with the sinker, treble hooks and flopping fish.

Tip: Summer fishing means you need to cover a lot of ground. Covering ground means trolling jigs, crankbaits or power trolling. Jigs and crankbaits get top billing, but power trolling also offers a boat-control technique that works great when wanting to follow contours.

CHAPTER 14
Easy/Versatile Setup...with Sinkers

Setup Note: This technique is moderately easy to learn and perform, very few additional setup costs. Effectiveness rating: 3 out of 10.

Wade Mansfield use to be a regular on the tournament trail but in recent years has spent more time tending the family business, the Grizzly Jig Company. Mansfield is also the publisher of Crappie Angler Magazine, the best hard-copy crappie fishing-magazine available.

On a past trip, he demonstrated that a quick modification for crankbaits is possible without redesigning or configuring the boat. This isn't the ideal crankbait setup, but for the occasional crankbaiter, it's a great way to pull without spending extra money or re-rigging a boat.

Equipment List
- Existing slow-trolling equipment that should include pole holders, poles and electronics.
- Crankbaits in a variety of colors.

As you can see from the equipment list, this incorporates crankbaits and existing equipment. Although this system is similar to the previous section, it's not the perfect system because it doesn't have holders at fixed spots for trolling crankbaits or specialized rods and reels.

The advantages include a less-expensive setup cost. Another advantage is fewer poles and other equipment in the boat even when planning to use two techniques.

"I never enjoyed pulling crankbaits," says Mansfield. "It just doesn't feel like fishing to me. I like to slow troll and jig fish. However, there are times when the crappie are scattered and it's necessary to adapt to catch fish."

Setup

Mansfield can stay in the front seat and use the same racks and poles he uses when slow trolling. "I don't want to carry a lot of extra equipment with me in the boat. I don't want extra pole holders and racks around my boat. I know I give up a little, but using the same equipment saves me money and makes things simple."

He gets to his trolling areas, turns his boat, starts the trolling motor and then feeds line out to the depth he wants on each pole. His rig includes a 1.5-ounce egg sinker he positions three feet above the crankbait.

Fishing

"I use the sinker system because I fish by myself a lot and it doesn't take as much line when using sinkers. If I catch a fish or have to stop for some other reason, I can get off the trolling motor and everything settles down without getting tangled up. Another advantage is turning more sharply than with long lines."

Depth control is simple. He counts the line out by hand. Because it takes less line, it's not a big deal. He also changes bait depth by varying the speed of his trolling motor. Unlike other methods, the slower he goes, the deeper the baits go because of the sinkers. He often starts by letting out 50 to 100 feet.

"I like to find the fish schooled up. They may be chasing schools of shad, held up over a channel or simply scattered about in open-water. I usually go with the wind because it's easier and helps my trolling motor batteries."

"My favorite colors are pink, chartreuse, red and black/chrome. The sun seems to make a big difference in the color they want. A bright sun usually triggers more bites."

Tips & Tricks

- A good net is important. The net doesn't need to be one that grabs and tangles crankbaits. The one made of rubber has the least tangles, but it's heavy and has a lot of water drag. Others are available that are more like the old nylon netting but are rubber-coated so hooks don't penetrate the material. There are still tangles because of the thinner netting and close weave, but hooks can be shaken or jiggled free. These nets are lighter weight and easier to handle.

- Equipment option: The Driftmaster Crows Foot lets you convert a bass-boat-style deck to a spider-rig deck without drilling a hole. They have a lot of adjustment to move holders from the front of the deck toward the sides.

Tip: Sometimes crankbaits have to be run shallow. Crappie will find a shallow flat in 8 or 10 feet of water that they like. The trick will be to avoid spooking fish with the boat and getting baits to the right depths without too many hangups. Trolling motors are best. Planers run off the side are best.

CHAPTER 15
Party Barge...Pulling & Pushing

Setup Note: This method is difficult to learn, difficult to perform and moderately expensive. The method can be simplified with fewer poles. Effectiveness rating: 6 out of 10.

Equipment List
- Party barge.
- Big motor with trolling plate. Big autopilot trolling motor with extra sets of batteries.
- 16-foot stiff poles out front; 7.5-foot stiff poles out sides.
- Baitcasters on front; line-counter reels on side.
- 10- to 17-pound-test line.
- 5-ounce sinkers for long poles.
- Bandit 300-series; or your favorite.

Setup

Why a party barge? A party barge gives a solid platform fishermen can walk around on. It's great for family and friends. Line separation is good on the big boat. Up to 14 poles can be used at one time without too many problems. It's a comfortable way to fish. A canopy provides shade and rain protection.

Shorter poles are on each side with the rodtips being higher in back and lower as they go to the front. Longpoles are placed across the front of the boat. They use 5-ounce sinkers four feet above the baits.

Fishing

Using a lot of poles allows you to find crappie quickly. Start by looking for vertical lines of fish in the 10- to 16-foot range on the locator. Once these lines are showing up on the locator, it's time to put out baits. Troll through the spot, but troll around other nearby spots to find other schools.

Short poles are staggered at different angles and lines are at slightly different lengths. Line length, boat speed and angle of the rod determine bait depth.

Long poles use heavy sinkers to keep baits as vertical as possible. Catching fish isn't much fun on the long poles, and there are some precautions you need to use. First, let out line, placing the sinker and crank toward the water. Place the pole in the holder. Raise the pole back up and measure your line in reference to the pole. Release the sinker and let the rig fall to the water.

There is a trick to catching, too. Leave the rod in the holder and place your left hand up on the pole. Then lift. When the crappie gets to the top, net it or swing it into the boat. When the bait, sinker and fish get within reach, you should grab the sinker with one hand and the fish with the other. Leave the pole alone. Put the bait back by grabbing the sinker and swinging it back out.

Long poles and long-lines give a one-two punch to provide action from a pontoon boat. No other boat is more comfortable or fun for several fishermen.

Tips & Tricks

- Don't set the hook on a vertical pole or long-line pole. It's tempting, but it'll rip the crank out of the crappie's mouth. The best thing to do on a short pole is grab the pole and remove it from the holder. Find the direction the fish is going so you can steer it away from the other lines. Hold the rod tip high and scoot the fish across the top of the water.
- The month of May through fall is often the best to both catch fish and enjoy the weather with friends and family on the deck of a pontoon.
- Weather usually isn't a major factor, but too much wind can make pontoon handling a problem.

- Speed is critical so try doing a figure eight to see what the fish want; faster on outside poles or slower on the inside poles.
- Start right by buying good quality. Buying cheap holders or poles only results in another purchase later to get equipment that works.
- **Note:** A better tactic can be to use offset poles on the side using an 18-, 14- and 10-footer; or 16-, 12- and 8-foot. Use a few long poles along the front. Sticking with 10 to 12 poles for three or four people will make fishing much easier.

Tip: Do not hesitate concentrating on river and creek channels in the summer. They are highways for the fish and provide deeper water. Crappie can come up on top of the ledges when feeding. Slow methods allow baits to be targeted to specific spots. However, fast trolling works great because baits must be crisscrossed over the top of a winding channel.

CHAPTER 16
Economy Trolling...
Pulling One or Two Poles

Setup Note: Easy to learn, easy to perform, basic setup is inexpensive. Effectiveness rating: 2 out of 10.

Equipment List
- Simple depth finder and GPS.
- Bass outfits makes good trolling poles. So do heavy-action long poles. Poles receive strong pulls and pressure from hang-ups and big fish so the poles must be able to withstand the pressure.
- Rod holders are not required for short periods of trolling. However, if you troll occasionally you'll want holders.
- Line should be 10- to 17-pound test.
- Crankbaits can vary.

Setup & Fishing

The good news is that you can troll crankbaits for crappie without doing a total rigging setup. Each person in the boat can hold one pole while trolling down the lake. Trolling is fun and relaxing if you're tired of other methods or just want to enjoy a little fishing without too much work. All that's required is to flip a crankbait over the side, let out an appropriate amount of line and troll.

You can troll with your big motor if it goes as slowly as needed for trolling, about 1.5 mph. You can also slow your boat by using five-gallon buckets or wind socks off the back of the boat. If not, you'll need to use your trolling motor. A GPS is needed keep the right speed and mark good areas.

Make trolling runs in water deep enough so the baits won't drag bottom or hangup in cover. Watch the locator for suspended fish and concentrate in these areas.

If you learn you like this method, the addition of two or three rod holders will make trolling more enjoyable for everyone in the boat.

This method is simple, easy and relaxing. The negatives are having only one bait in the water and not knowing the exact depth unless you count each pull of line. However, it is fun fishing and a lot of species will be caught, including crappie.

Tip: Above everything else, it's critical to stay healthy on the water. Summer heat can lead to serious, permanent problems. Keep skin protected and stay hydrated. Damp towels from a cooler placed around your neck are good cooling aids. Use an umbrella during high sun. Fish early before the heat (and pleasure boaters) becomes a problem.

NOTES

CHAPTER 17
Casting Crankbaits

Casting is in a totally different category than anything previously mentioned. It's a hit or miss based upon finding good cover or finding schools of shad being chased by crappie.

Several serious crappie fishermen like to toss crankbaits to potential, or known, crappie spots. Crankbaits are something different for the crappie and can target some of the biggest fish in a spot or area.

Clearer-water lakes seem to produce best, but crappie can be caught from any lake. One trick is to target single covers like a single stickup, a big rock, bridge piling or anything else where it's easy to get a crankbait. Of course the bigger brushpiles and covers also are likely to produce fish but will be more difficult to fish without hang-ups.

Fish will hit lipless cranks, blade-type cranks and others, but larger-lipped baits are usually best. Baits like a Deep Little N, Bandit 300 and Flicker Shad are samples of good baits. A wildcard but good choice is a minnow crank Rogue. These allow more stops, pauses and erratic motions to be applied.

Bass fishermen using larger baits say it's not uncommon to catch one to three big crappie a day while bass fishing. Large cranks, spinners and plastics catch few crappie, but the ones caught are good ones. By downsizing baits, it's logical to believe these big fish still can be caught along with more midsize fish.

Tips & Tricks

- **Winter crankbait casting tip:** Side Scan to find fish suspended over brushpiles out in open-water. You can throw a jerkbait, like a 4.5-inch Lucky Craft, and crank to the fish. The tactic can be dynamite.
- Open water winter action! A school of shad usually indicates a spot to catch crappie with the crankbait. Simply cast past or into the school and hard jerkbait back to the boat with very long pauses. You'll catch crappie until the shad school is spooked away.

Tip: Don't forget to have fun when fishing. We sometimes get too wrapped up in doing a technique or setting some other goal causing fishing to become work instead of fun. Don't forget to set aside some time to relax, be thankful for your day on the water and enjoy the moment.

CHAPTER 18
Crankbaiting Miscellaneous

More Tips & Tricks: Longlining

- Reel counters are a key tool for serious trolling, but marking your line with a Magic Marker when action is fast makes resetting much easier. You can let line out until you get to the marked line instead of watching a reel counter.
- Running lines parallel makes it easier to see when you have a fish because the line will rise, giving it a different angle than the others. High-visibility line is critical.
- You can catch fish on ledges, but the long lines make open-water trolling much easier. Long lines and lagging baits make staying on a ledge difficult, but crossing back and forth across the ledge (while trolling a straight path) is usually very good.
- Use electronics to find crappie stacked on top of each other. These suspended fish are most likely to bite.

- They may be on top of each other or staggered like a staircase on the locator.
- Baits can't run on bottom or in cover because of hang-ups. Paying attention to depths and structure is critical when pulling cranks.
- Deeper water around a dam is an excellent place to try. The hotter the water, the more likely crappie will be on the deepest part of the lake.
- Using the big motor isn't popular in today's fishing because of autopilot trolling motors. But the big motor removes the worry of batteries running down or having to recharge at a motel if traveling. A small kicker motor is ideal for speed control and quietness.
- A hooked crappie will come to the surface and can be skidded across the surface of the water. A really large fish has a lot of water resistance, therefore, a lot of pressure on the hooks. It's good to kick the motor out of gear until the fish is in the boat.
- A line swivel is required. It eliminates twist especially when a catfish comes in like a helicopter.

Summer Structure: Deep Flats

Temperatures were pushing triple digits as we deployed the umbrella. We were moving along at 2.0 miles per hour. Our procedure included wiping sweat, talking, laughing and watching poles. The rod tips were vibrating as the baits did their work. We were interrupted many times that day by poles bending when a crappie would take our crankbait. Deep flats were ignored for years by most anglers, but today's crankbait fishermen have made them important structures for catching summer crappie.

The Flat. Any depth flat can be fished, but, in the summer, choose 20 feet or deeper when possible. A flat may have varying degrees of change in the bottom with small drops, channels, humps and dips. However, for fishing purposes, these irregularities can be ignored. Summer crappie like relating to these spots, but they will be suspended over them.

Flats may have cover. Stumps or small beds are fine, but they need to be deeper than the depth the crankbaits are running or many hang-ups will occur.

Finding flats can be done with a contour map, electronic map and locator.

Summer Factors

Wind: The great thing about crankbaits is that wind does not prevent you from catching crappie. Due to boat control, windy days are best fished with two people so one can attend the motor; or, have an automatic-type trolling motor. The auto-trolling motors may be the best items ever invented for fast trollers. They can be set to a direction, then all attention can be given to the poles.

Sun/Rain: It's impossible to predict for sure. However, crappie will move up in the water or down dependent upon sunlight penetration. Sunny, hot days are often best for cranks.

Current: This is usually a bad factor for crankbaiting because fish will move tight to cover. Crappie need to be located out in open-water.

Heat: The hotter it is, the better the fishing. This is one technique that often gets better in the middle of the day. However, for the health of the fisherman, early morning is usually the best time to fish in mid-summer.

Fishing Pressure: This is typically not a problem in summer. However, when there are fisherman along with pleasure boaters, it makes maneuvering along a specific area a problem.

Boating Pressure: Recreational boaters, skiers and jet skis are a nuisance and can make fish go down to the bottom and/or quit biting. But everyone has a right to the lake, so be tolerant and fish early morning.

Boat Steering

Console Steering: Most boats have consoles. These work fine for trolling. A big motor needs a trolling plate. Pole racks should be forward so you can watch from behind the steering wheel. (This method has rapidly declined due to the popularity of auto-trolling motors).

Tiller Control: Tiller-control motors allow many advantages and work well for trolling. A tiller generally means a smaller boat, so there is less initial cost, and they are economical to operate. Tiller motors are quick and give better control. No console means more room in the boat. Pole holders with a tiller are usually in the middle to rear portion of the boat. Tillers have disadvantages but are often good choices for economical fishing.

Trolling Motor: Poles on the side of the boat can be difficult to handle with a foot-controlled trolling motor. An autopilot-style motor is a great addition. For a serious troller, an autopilot is a necessity.

Best Crankbait Colors

Experts have trouble explaining why crappie are so color sensitive to crankbaits. The baits are moving fast, yet colors are critical. Best colors change day-to-day and hour-to-hour. The following list of colors came from interviewing a number of fishermen.

- Pink. The overwhelming favorite color was a lighter pink shade with sparkles. Other pinks are next.
- Orange. Several years ago, orange became the rage, and it's still catching crappie today.
- Chartreuse and chartreuse with any color.
- Chrome-black and chrome-blue.

- Black, black-purple and firetiger. Dark colors are a "must have".
- Shad colors, red crawfish and mad cow makes up the remainder of the group. The shad colors rank near the top in clear lakes.
- Many other combinations, including browns, purples, yellows, white and greens, were given as excellent baits on certain days but not consistent producers.

Crankbaits to Try

Bandit 200 and 300 series; Lucky Craft; Berkley Flicker Shad; Storm Wiggle Wart; Rapala JSR5; Mann's 15; Bomber Fat Free Fingerling or Model 6A; Strike King 200 and 300 series; and Johnson Crappie Buster.

CHAPTER 19
Summer Tips: No Crankbaits

- Mississippi guide Vic Finkley says summer spider rigging can be good. "Fishing here can be in deeper 14- to 16-foot waters. The crappie are out on the flats following baitfish. Just follow the bait and you'll find the crappie. I use a Humminbird graph to find the bait and crappie."
- Double-hook rigs with a short top leader. Finkley says, "Try spider rigging with double-hook rigs. I usually use a double jig rig with MidSouth jigs tipped with minnows. My weight is 1/2-ounce with jigs about 18 inches apart. Go with a short leader on top so you'll feel more bites. A long leader allows a fish to swim around with the bait without showing a bite. He can't do it with a short leader."
- Finkley says, "I use 16-foot BnM Pro Staff poles. These are hard for clients who aren't use to using long poles. They'll reel the fish up to the tip and wonder what to do next. But the longer poles make

a difference in the number of bites we get. I recommend anyone who wants to be serious about spider rigging to get the longest pole they are comfortable using."

- Find the shade. "In the summer, the fish will quit in the middle of the day in some of the open-water areas," says Dan Dannenmueller. "It's mainly due to lack of shade. When the side of a channel is shaded, the crappie will come up and bite. The sun changes position and puts that side of the channel into the sun, and they quite biting. A good tip is to try the other side of the channel. The crappie will change sides to get into the shade. We learned this and have found it to work in several situations when fishing in the summer.

- "In August when fish start transitioning, they will be in some of the same places they were located during post-spawn. In the mornings when the water is a few degrees cooler and the sun is low, the crappie will likely be shallower. As the sun comes up, the fish will go back down to mid-depth water. The fish might get tight to cover, but more likely they'll be suspended out near a drop, cover or other specific structure," says Dannenmueller.

- Look shallow. Kevin Jones, a good tournament fisherman from Missouri, says he is spider rigging in the summer. "I enjoy vertical jigging, but spider rigging is the most productive technique. The fish, especially on a lake like Truman, will move into 3 to 5 feet of water. The shallow fish are much easier to catch and keep alive when fishing a tournament so we target these fish. Recreational fishermen can use the same strategy."

- Look deep. Kevin Jones says, "Deep fish in 15 to 20 feet of water are different than shallow because it's not unusual to catch 50 fish off the deeper cover. One brushpile can be loaded. Spider rigging with live bait is the best way to catch these fish. It's fun, but these fish will die after you catch them, so have a cooler to put them in."
- Live bait or jigs? Kevin Jones says, "We use Muddy Water Baits, but we also use live bait. We tip jigs with minnows. The minnows are great even when the fish aren't biting because, if you leave it in front of their face long enough, they'll usually decide to hit it. If we know fish are in a brushpile and just turned off, we might stay at a brushpile for 30 minutes to get the fish to bite."
- Look for the biggest brushpiles. Jones last tip is a good one to remember. "In the summer the fish are tight to cover, so we spider rig but sit still on the brush. The larger brushpiles usually hold the biggest

and most crappie, so we look for big tops with a lot of mass and area."

- Sit Still. Fisherman Loren Nelms, former Johnson Fishing pro staff member, says, "Summer presentations depend upon how the fish are located on the cover. We will set up on top of them if we have to, but we'll also get pretty fast sometimes. Summer means fishing right in the cover, so we will be set up to spider rig, but when we get to the cover we'll stop and leave the baits there so we won't hang up, and we'll give the fish time to bite."

- Keep baits over the fish. Nelms says, "One mistake a lot of fishermen make is fishing under the fish. Their baits are too deep. Never fish under crappie. Start baits shallow and work down in the water column. If you drop down too quickly, you may miss the fish up high in the water."

CHAPTER 20
Fall

Limiting Out!!

Learning a pattern is the key to catching numbers of fish in the fall. Find the fish and you'll have no trouble filling your livewell. Shad schools may be your key to success.

Terms to Know (Fall)
- Lake Turnover: A time when the upper, cooler layer of water goes to the bottom due to being heavier than the warmer water below. The mixing of waters causes poor oxygen levels, bad pH and adds bottom junk (leaves, mud, etc.) to the water. It's the time to stay home.
- Oxbow: An old riverbed usually separated from the main river except during times of flooding.
- Visibility: A measure of water clarity. Example: at what water depth does a jig disappear? General rule-of-thumb guidelines: muddy is less than two feet;

stained is greater than two feet; clear is greater than four or five feet; ultra-clear is greater than eight or ten feet.

Key Facts & Concepts (Fall)

- Crappie are on the move in fall, so you should be, too. Don't stay in a spot where you're not catching fish. Keep moving until you find them.
- Lake turnover is the toughest time of the year to get a bite.
- Wood is typically an excellent cover in the fall.
- Fall crappie will be located in areas similar to springtime yet situated just a little deeper.
- Crappie will follow schools of baitfish.

Fall Migration

Fall is a great time for sportsmen. The air temperatures are cooling, hunting seasons are opening, fall leaves paint the sky, and fish are on the move. It's a great combination and a wonderful season for outdoorsmen.

Stage 1, The Gradual Change: Crappie migration begins with summer crappie scattered and suspended in some lakes, while other lakes have fish loosely holding to specific structures. As water temperatures start to cool and daylight hours decrease, crappie realize changes are taking place and it's time to move.

During this late summer/early fall period, techniques can vary with slow trolling and float-and-fly being two good choices. Slow trolling allows any depth to be fished. Also, fish are likely to want different presentations in the fall, with slow trolling offering anything from being stopped to a relatively fast speed. When crappie are on schools of baitfish instead of cover, the technique is good for following them.

The float/fly (float/jig) is good when fish are in shallow-water. This casting tactic allows the boat to stay a long distance from the fish so they won't spook. Fancasting is a good way to locate the best concentrations of fish, and then repeated casts let you have lots of fun pulling in spunky crappie.

A wildcard tactic is pulling crankbaits. You can use your trolling motor or idle with the big motor to pull baits along drops and flats between deep and shallow-water. This tactic is good until water cools in late fall.

Stage 2, Cooling: As water temperatures continue to cool, the fish move to the mouths of creeks and big coves from the main river channels and deep holes. Their direction is often toward spawning site areas used in spring.

During this stage, look for crappie to be at a variety of depths. Fish might be at five feet today and 10 feet tomorrow. Also, their depths can vary a lot during the day as temperatures and light penetration vary.

Stage 3, Active Feeding: When water nears 70 degrees, another period is in full swing. This is a good time because the fish are aggressive, and they are often found around cover in shallow and mid-depth water. Watch your locator for cover and fish. Also watch for schools of shad. Pay special attention at bends, points or other irregular features. It may take time to find the fish, but the action can be excellent when you locate them. During this period, it is best to stay on the move until numbers of fish are found.

Stage 4, Turnover: This period is not a migration as much as a time of confusion. You can recognize the turnover by dirty, nasty water without a rain or runoff causing it. Fish are looking for good water with oxygen, so fishing is terrible for a week or two.

If you do go fishing, concentrate on finding some pockets of good water. You can do this visually and by watching the locator. When you see a big concentration of fish, be sure to drop a bait to them.

Stage 5, The Final Move: The last migration of the season is when the water cools to between 50 and 59 degrees. The fish move toward their winter homes, often in mid-depth or shallower water, depending upon the lake. Fish are forming tight groups during this period, and they aggressively feed.

CHAPTER 21
Naturally Stained Water

Fall can be as productive as spring. Crappie will move in a pattern similar to the spring. They'll be chasing shad at every opportunity. It's a peaceful time to fish because there are fewer people on the lake and you're not fighting the traffic.

The fall patterns are similar to springtime. When the water becomes stained, the fish often get tighter to cover. It's important to keep the cover in mind when searching for fall fish.

Slow trolling and vertical jigging both work, but catching fish jigging is certainly more fun than watching a pole tip. But technique is a personal preference, so whatever a fisherman likes is fine. However, comparing the two techniques, the odds are much better for slow trolling because four poles with two baits each means a fisherman has eight baits in the water instead of one.

One of the best patterns for vertical jigging is visible cover. Brush piles and laydowns are good, and many get overlooked because in the fishermen's minds it's been fished to death. But the visible cover can be easy to fish and productive.

Stained water is an advantage because fish are less spooky and you can get closer to them. That's critical because, if the fish know a fisherman is there, the game is over. Little things like keeping your shadow off the cover you're fishing, not throwing trolling motor backwash or making too much noise are all negative factors when jigging.

Also, when fishing vertical wood cover, make sure to keep your jig as close as possible to the wood. You can work it away from the cover, but start with the jig hugging the main cover.

CHAPTER 22
Texas-Style Fishing

"It's easier to catch fish in the fall because they get in a pattern," says Mr. Crappie, Wally Marshall, a Texas resident. "Once you figure the pattern, they will be in large schools. You can catch big numbers of fish. It's a fun time that makes it all worthwhile.

"In a creek, they'll start relating to cover. In open water, they'll be in deep water chasing schools of shad. In Texas the magic number is 30 feet. Temperatures are still good there."

Marshall says there is one key tip to help fishermen catch more fish…don't stay too long in one place when you're not catching fish. Stay on the move until you find a productive spot. There is no reason to fish where you're not catching. Stay on the move until you find them, then slow down.

Marshall slow trolls. It's the best method for presenting baits slowly in deep water. He uses his Wally Marshall/Mr. Crappie products, line in 10-pound-test high-vis, 14-foot signature-series poles and Blakemore Slab Daddy jigs.

Fishing at 30 feet, he uses two jigs in tandem, separating them 15 to 20 inches. He also adds minnows when the bite is tough.

CHAPTER 23
Oxbows

Each oxbow has a unique personality. Some are almost bare, while others have snags, weeds and manmade structure. Also, river levels can be a critical factor for good or bad fishing. So fishing patterns will need to be adjusted to the water conditions and oxbow characteristics. The following are some general guidelines to fishing an oxbow in the fall.

"Oxbow fall patterns are not unlike spring patterns," says Scott Stafford from Missouri. "The fish will move into shallower water as the water cools. If you know how to fish in the spring, you'll have no trouble adjusting a little, and catching fish in the fall.

"On a normal year, the water level will be up in the spring and then go down throughout the year. Fishing is best in the spring and fall, with fishing success usually determined by the water conditions. Stable water is important. Anything else makes the bite very tough.

"Oxbows have tiny ledges that are formed by current during flooding. A few oxbows stay landlocked, but most will have current flow when the river gets up. The ledge can be a foot or less in height. It doesn't take much for a crappie to find and use it.

"Next, you need to find a blow-down across the break, and you have a great place to catch fish. You can place money on a spot like that. Crappie are shallow in the spring in connection to the spawn, but they are there in the fall to feed on baitfish that go shallow. Most of the fishing will be in water 6 feet or less."

Stafford says he likes a black/chartreuse jig in the tinted water. Of course, you can use minnows, and they work well to catch crappie, but oxbows have a tremendous number of gar. If you're trolling for crappie, he says, you'll need at least two or three times the number of minnows than you think you'll need just because of the gar.

CHAPTER 24
Clear Water

Clear-water lakes vary depending upon depth and other factors, but most fish catching is difficult in the summer and picks up dramatically in the fall. Clear-water fishing is different because crappie are spookier and special tactics are often required for best results.

The first clear-water tactic is slow trolling. Some fishermen say this is not a good tactic because fish can see the boat before they see the baits. This is true when using standard equipment, but switching to 16- or 20-foot poles can make this an outstanding method.

Slow trolling has the advantage of keeping multiple baits in the strike zone all the time. Any depth water can be fished, and any bait, or bait combination, can be used. The rule of thumb is to use smaller baits in clearer water.

Jigging is another good tactic in clear water. Many years ago, I watched Jim Coleman and his partner catch their crappie during a day-two Crappie USA Classic on Patoka Lake, Indiana. They were jigging the timber using very slow presentations and small minnows. Jim's method resulted in a classic championship. The clear water did not prevent them from catching fish by jigging.

Jigging deeper water can include standard pole length, but in shallow and mid-depths, it's wise to use a longer 14- or 16-foot pole for crappie. Jigs are the preferred bait because they are easier to present in the brush. However, in clear water where fish visibility is very good, a small, lively minnow can be more productive.

Long-lining is a third method for fishing clear lakes in the fall. It's especially good in the wind. Bait bounce is not an issue because of the long lines. The choppy surface adds oxygen to the water, and fish are less spooky. Without going into details of the technique, it's important to mention that most experts prefer 4-pound-test line for both depth control and to avoid spooking crappie with the line. Trolling baits include any action tail. Road Runner heads with silver blades are a popular with trollers.

CHAPTER 25
Intersections

October and November crappie fishing can be outstanding. Although hunting seasons may overshadow the fishing, real crappie fishermen know crappie are cooperative right now. An intersection is a good place to find these fish. Here are a few types of intersections for fall and early-winter crappie.

When you think "intersection," your mind likely moves to a creek/river or channel/bank intersection. These can be great spots for finding crappie but there are many other connecting spots that work.

Why is a channel intersection important? Because it's where two channels meet. Think about our highways. Cars run up and down the highways. Where two major highways meet is where you'll have the most cars. Fish use channel ledges and other structures like we use highways. Therefore, a good spot to expect heavier-than-normal crappie numbers is where two or more of these meet.

Contour maps make these spots easy to find. Hard copies work great but so do the electronic maps that can be used on the water in conjunction with your boat position. The trick is to do your homework to find these spots.

When you reach an intersection, it's important to look for key hotspots. A point formed by two of the channel legs might be a top spot. A stump row on the top ledge might be another. Because every intersection is different, each one must be inspected with electronics.

The key to catching more crappie is learning a pattern. A pattern is simply learning the right depths, covers and presentations to catch fish. If you learn that fish are on the downstream side of an intersection in 13 feet of water and relating to stumps, you have found a pattern. You can find other similar spots, fish them the same way and expect similar successful results. By targeting high percentage pattern spots, you catch more fish by not wasting time in non-productive water.

Late-season crappie often starts in shallow and mid-depth waters when they are chasing shad. Depending upon whether you are in the South, North or somewhere between, your search can begin in waters four to 12 feet. Adjust to the crappie. As the water cools, crappie will usually go deeper in 12 to 30 feet. So match your searches to the right depths.

Slow Trolling Intersections

The modern setup for slow trolling is to use 14-foot poles, quality rod holders and double-hook bait rigs. A fisherman can use jigs, minnows or combinations. A foot-controlled trolling motor is the best for slow trolling.

Slow trolling allows you to move quickly while searching and then slow down or stop when you find the right spot. Two to four poles give you multiple opportunities to be at different depths and to use different baits.

One advanced trick is to find a brushpile on a ledge where wind is blowing toward deeper water. Move the boat slowly from deeper water into the drop-off. When baits hit cover or a fish is caught, let off the trolling motor to allow the wind blow you away from the cover and ledge. This prevents a bunch of baits from being forced into the brush and hung up because wind blows the boat away from, not into, the cover. It's not difficult but a fisherman has to pay attention to get the right setup.

Casting

The intersections mentioned above usually can be fished by casting. The first step is to find the fish because casting isn't a good search method. Take time to check out the area and pinpoint with GPS and/or marker buoys where you want to cast. A bottom changing from rocks to mud or a set of stumps on the point of the intersection are examples of where you want to cast.

Cast directly to the intersection. Curly-tail and paddle-tail jigs are top picks because they have action when retrieved.

The look and vibration are good triggers for bites. Charlie Brewer Slider, Spike-It, Southern Pro and Bobby Garland are a few examples.

Work different depths to look for fish and cover. Be sure to get baits to the best spots. A spot should only take a few minutes to test-fish. Leave if you don't get bites, but stay if you do. If you're successful, try to find other similar locations. They are likely to produce similar results.

Casting may not be the most productive fall method, but when it works, it's a barrel of fun. Going one-on-one with a crappie is a great way to get the adrenaline active. Keep a distance from the fish to avoid spooking them, cast, retrieve and set the hook.

Other Casting Tips

- Don't be afraid to change jig colors until you find what the crappie like best. Also, try different length baits to match the baitfish.
- Tip a jig with a minnow when fishing is tough. Casting with a minnow is not ideal, but the real flash, smell and look of the minnow can trigger more strikes.
- Casting can include a slip-float minnow rig. It allows you to pull or drift the minnow into the key areas. The bobber stop can be set to the exact zone you want.

- Fish different depth zones. If in shallow or mid-depth water, you can let your jig fall until it rests on bottom, then retrieve it slowly with short hops.
- One of the secrets of successful casting is being able to repeat casts to a sweet spot. In open water, this is almost impossible. Use a marker buoy for reference. Throw it close but not on the cover.

Vertical Jigging

Standing timber can be excellent for vertical jigging during the fall. Is wood cover considered to be an intersection? No, but timber can have intersections within a tree. Any spot where a tree has a limb going out from the trunk is an intersection. The first and largest limbs are likely to be the best spots. For some reason, the biggest crappie like to claim the biggest spots.

Vertical jigging lets you fish straight up and down with a minimum of hang-ups. This popular technique allows you to check intersections you find in the wood. Do not ignore the spots mentioned or others you find. Maybe the snag you're fishing has another snag leaning against it underwater. That's an obvious intersection. Finding less obvious ones are what separates some of the best fishermen from the others, so pay attention to details.

Other intersections? How about bridge pilings with horizontal members. They create intersections. A fence row of trees is a roadblock that intersects a crappie's travel path across a flat.

Every lake is different. It's up to you to find intersections and use the best method for fishing them. You will be rewarded for your efforts.

Summary

- Intersections: They are everywhere. Many are easy to visualize or see while others are less obvious. Some we notice and just take for granted, like a creek channel and river channel intersection. Start in the fall by fishing intersections at four to 12 feet in stained waters. Fish usually go deeper as the water gets cold.
- Techniques: Many methods are good, but casting is one that is both fun and productive. Slow trolling has the best odds for good numbers of fish.
- Tackle: Moderate-priced equipment works fine for catching crappie as described above. Quality 6-pound-test line is good for most situations. Heavier cover might require 8-pound-test or braid. Baits can be varied to match the situation and to what crappie prefer on a particular day.
- When/where: Look for intersections anywhere you can find them. Start in about eight feet of water in stained lakes and work shallower or deeper as required.

CHAPTER 26
Fall Turnover

"You're a hero or a zero in my part of the country in the fall," says Oklahoma guide Huckabee. "Turnover changes everything and usually means that you may fish a long time to find the fish because there is so much sour water with a low oxygen level, but when you find the fish they'll all be together. Fishing is phenomenal. Once you find them, you can quickly get your limit."

The situation is far from perfect. Water is so bad that holding areas Huckabee mentions are small, and there are very few of them. "I fish almost every day on my home lake, but it might take me six hours to find them. What's bizarre is that they are likely to be in 22 feet of water or at two feet. You never know where the best oxygen level will be for them. A windy day will add oxygen to shallow-water, so they might come up to the better water. Finding fall turnover fish can be difficult."

Huckabee says water was terrible during one of the fall tournaments he fished. The turnover had junked-up the

water and depleted oxygen levels. He finally found crappie hugging the bottom at 20 feet in a small layer of good water. The spot was loaded because that was the only good water in the area.

A couple weeks following turnover, fishing improves dramatically. Huckabee looks for fish to be in patterns similar to spring. The crappie are gorging for winter and must eat. They are also forming eggs, so they need food.

"I prefer to fish with a single pole and single jig. When they are in standing timber or deep water, it's a good way to fish. When they are in shallower cover, we'll back off and flip a slip-float so we won't get hung up or get the boat too close and spook them.

"There may be 300 fish in an area the size of a bathtub. Due to competition for food, when you find the numbers of fish, they'll attack a bait quickly. Again, these fish will likely be near cover."

He uses his Signature Series 10-foot pole and 10-pound-test Yo-Zuri Hybrid. His jig is a 1/8- or 1/4-ounce jig.

NOTES

CHAPTER 27

Seasonal Structure... Visible Wood Structure

Although it's true that fall crappie are moving, they often need a place to hold and rest. It's like us on vacation when we're traveling but want to stay at a motel for a few days. Wood cover makes an excellent crappie motel.

A stump, dock piling, laydown or any other piece of wood is a magnet for crappie. Fish can hide from predators, but the crappie are predators, too, as they wait in hiding for a baitfish to swim by.

Fishing Tactics: Your technique can vary based upon the depth and type cover. For example, slow trolling is a great technique when fish are on submerged wood with an occasional exposed stump or snag. This tactic allows you fish multiple baits in a slow, methodical fashion or kick up the speed a little to search.

One slow-trolling method when fishing a visible piece of wood cover is to take your outside pole out of the pole holder and work it around the wood. Your other poles will still be in the strike zone, but you increase your odds of a bite with the handheld pole by putting the bait right into a prime spot.

Vertical jigging is a top pick for visible wood. You and the crappie are in a one-on-one battle. You can invade his hangouts by vertical jigging. There is nothing like feeling a thump and setting the hook on a big slab.

Vertical jigging allows you to fish different depths and all sides of the cover. You can leave a bait still for a long time or keep it moving while looking for more aggressive fish. Once you learn the depth and preferred action, you can target only the prime spots thereby eliminating a lot of low-percentage places.

Jigs are the best baits to use when crappie will hit them. Vertical jigging is somewhat aggressive, and wood cover is bad about grabbing hooks, especially minnow hooks. Jigs are easier to handle with fewer hang-ups. You'll also catch more fish because you can catch two fish on a jig in the time it takes to re-bait a minnow and get it into the water. When bites are a little tough to get, one trick is to combine a leadhead with a minnow. You still get the advantages of a minnow but with more control by using a jighead.

Casting can be done when fishing visible cover when it is scattered. Cast past the cover and bring the bait next to the wood. Casting keeps you at a distance from the fish, making it a big advantage when crappie are shallow and spooky.

Don't be afraid of wood cover. No matter which technique you use, let the bait bump the cover. Whether it's the noise or the flaking off of algae or some other reason, crappie are often excited by this. Probably the best situation is when a jig drops off a horizontal limb.

The fall season can be unpredictable, but many experts talk about the good fishing, comfortable weather and less-crowded lakes. Crappie migrate into and out of shallower and mid-depth water, so be prepared to do a little searching. When you see baitfish in an area, it's time to intensify your search in that location.

Tip: Fall is a great time of year. There are fewer cold fronts than in spring. The weather is beautiful and so are the fall colors. Oxygen is getting back into the water, so fish are moving and active. Find the fish and you'll find the action.

CHAPTER 28
Fall Factors & Tips

Wind: You'll have less wind in the fall compared to the spring. However, having a few good spots no matter which direction the wind is blowing will guarantee a place to fish.

Water Temperatures: Slowly cooling water causes fish to become more active and go to shallow or mid-depth water to feed. Be sure to pay attention to water temperature because a change of two degrees can be huge for finding crappie.

Water Color: The actual color of the water isn't as important as being stable. Stable water, even if it is muddy, means fish are adjusted and will likely bite. Stained water is easier to fish than clear water because fish are not as spooky.

Cold Front: A strong front creates a bad situation. After it passes, the crappie may be in a negative feeding mood for a while. Bright sun following a front means a tough bite. Fortunately, there are fewer cold fronts in fall than in spring.

Current: Fall rainfall is usually light to moderate, so water flow won't be a problem in most large lakes and reservoirs. When current is present, look for crappie to hold behind current breaks or in backwaters.

Fishing Pressure: The good thing about fall is much less fishing pressure because pleasure boats are gone and hunting season is in progress.

Question: How macro can crappie baits get?

- John Harrison from Mississippi says he uses a 1/16-ounce a lot for typical fishing but, "I have gone to a larger 3/8-ounce jighead when going for big slabs, a large 2-inch Southern Pro Umbrella and a three or four inch minnow. I'm looking for one big bite."
- Brad Whitehead says, "I've caught crappie on Pickwick with 4- and 4.5-inch baitfish in them. I've been trolling big crankbaits in late summer and fall to catch crappie."
- Barry Morrow, a guide in Oklahoma and Missouri, says, "Aggressive fish will eat anything. I clean them with a 4-inch shad in them. We see some big baitfish."

Question: If you could only have one jig in the boat, what would it be?

- Don Collins, tournament fisherman, says, "A Pro Series Road Runner, chartreuse head, 1/8-ounce, with a blue-white Crappie Thunder Body."
- Barbara Reedy, tournament fisherman from Missouri, says, "One jig. That would be a chartreuse Pro Series Road Runner with a willow-leaf blade, 1/32-ounce, with a lime-green MidSouth tube."
- Freddie Gilliland says, "1/8-ounce leadhead, lime-chartreuse Bobby Garland Slab Buster."
- John Harrison says, "1/16-ounce head with Gamakutsu hook, orange-chartreuse, 2-inch Southern Pro tube."
- Others mentioned: MidSouth glow lemon-lime with a black 1/16-ounce jighead; Grizzly Goggle-Eye, 1/16-ounce, in black-chartreuse; Southern Pro pink-chartreuse Hot Grub on a 1/16-ounce red head; Bobby Garland in shad color or lime-chartreuse; the jig you have the most confidence in.

Other Fall Tips

- It's okay to use a big bait but don't forget to try a smaller offer if fishing is tough.

- One fisherman caught a tiny crappie on a 300-Bandit. The fish was not hooked but didn't have enough weight to pull out the treble hook wedged in its mouth. So, it makes you wonder, how big can baits get?
- Many fishermen believe crappie will hit a 3- or 4-inch bait, but most fishermen won't fish a bait that large. So, here is a question to you: If you could only have one jig in the boat, what would it be?

Tip: Crappie go into a fall feeding frenzy in shallow to mid-depth water. The arrival of winter and colder nights pushes fish out toward deeper water. As the water continues to cool, many crappie will set up winter homes along ledges in whatever depth has the most food and protection. Using electronics to scan ledges during cold months is an excellent method for finding fish.

CHAPTER 29
Winter

Limiting Out!!!

Winter is the best time of year to consistently catch a limit of quality fish. Experts agree that "slow" is a key when presenting baits. Downsizing is important, too.

Terms to Know
- Black Crappie: The two common crappie are black and white. The black has random dark spots, seven or eight spines at the front of the dorsal fin and is more football shaped with a thicker body. Black crappie weighs more per inch than white. They are known for their aggressiveness and fun fight.
- 214EL Hook: This hook has become the standard for crappie fishing whether fishing a single- or double-hook rig. The complete name is Eagle Claw 214 Extra-Light wire hook.

- Rosy-Red Minnow: This minnow is as slick as grease due to its very tight scale pattern. Its pinkish-orange color often attracts crappie, especially in stained water. The rosy red is a tough minnow, lasting much longer on the hook than a shiner.

Key Facts & Concepts
- The best winter baits are often smaller with less action.
- Winter bites can be extremely light. Use of sensitive line and equipment is best.
- Many fishermen are surprised to learn that winter crappie will make moves into shallow-water.

Winter Crappie

A cold-blooded crappie slows down when the water gets cold. It often holds in the same areas for long periods of time. Fortunately for fishermen, it doesn't quit eating just because it is cold. When you put a bait next to one, it will inhale it. The trick is to make slow presentations right in front of its nose.

Shallow Winter Fishing

Brent Work, former Reelfoot Lake guide, says he likes all seasons, but winter fishing is probably his favorite primarily because it's the best fishing. My trip was him was several years ago, but it's still deep in my memory. He says the tactics used then are all still good today.

"It surprises people that I fish shallow-water all year long," says Work. "In the winter, I'm often in five to six feet. The crappie's metabolism is real slow and so is my technique. I anchor and fish a spot for five or 10 minutes then pick up the anchor and move up a few feet and do it again. The slow presentation works."

His equipment includes 16-foot Wally Marshall poles with Shakespeare reels. The long pole is important to avoid spooking the shallow fish with the boat. He has a homemade rack to fit his boat with sturdy holders mounted on it for his poles.

"I tie my own crappie rigs with hooks about 24 inches apart. I use various weights, from 1/4 to 1/2 ounce. I use Eagle Claw 214 Extra-Light Wire hooks with heavier line so the hooks straighten right out. I use 20-pound Suffix most of the time so I won't be retying all the time. Sometimes I slide tubes up on the hooks to add color. I also use Grizzly Jigs and Sliders. I like green/chartreuse, pumpkinseed, blue/white, blue/chartreuse and red/white."

Work uses floats. The floats are good because it's easier to watch for bites. The floats are more sensitive than just watching the rod tip. He doesn't leave much slack line between the rod tip and the float, so the floats stay close together but don't get tangled with each other.

Winter fishing is cold, but Work says it's worth it. He catches bigger fish, and, most of the time, he catches black crappie. He stays warm by dressing in layers and uses a heater when necessary. He says there are fewer people, so it's more serene on the lake.

"To match their slow metabolism, I give them time to bite. I fish with both rosy red and shiner minnows, but prefer the shiners. I've gone to a bigger minnow, and the result is I catch fewer but bigger fish."

What does a bite look like? "Long poles are a disadvantage to handle, but I believe the 16-foot poles provide more bites because they get baits away from the boat. The long poles and short lines are a problem to handle. It's usually best to hand-over-hand them back until you can reach the line. The butt of the pole may be sticking in the water, but that's okay."

Work says it's common to get the boat on top of stumps at Reelfoot. He recommends just powering over them. Sometimes you have to transfer weight from the front to the back. A push pole can help. He uses a heavy, stable aluminum 1860 McBride boat powered by a shallow-water Go-Devil motor.

CHAPTER 30

Shallow-Water Casting

Garry Mason, founder and owner of Legends of the Outdoors Hall of Fame, a former Kentucky Lake crappie/bluegill guide, college bass coach and tourism director, says there is a specific weather condition that makes shallow-water casting excellent in the winter.

"A bright, sunshiny day with little or no wind is the time to look for shallow crappie. The fish move up as the minnows move up into the warmer water. We are talking two and three feet of water. It's almost unbelievable to most fishermen who are used to fishing 20 feet deep in the winter."

Mason says the key is that shallow-water can warm up five degrees during the day. "The baitfish move to the shallower water. The crappie follow the food source; kind of like me being drawn to a buffet."

Garry says the air temperature isn't critical because he catches fish with this pattern whether it's 35 degrees or 55 degrees. The key times are 9:30 in the morning until 3:30 in the afternoon.

Mason's equipment includes a BnM Sam Heaton 7-foot pole, Johnny Morris Bass Pro Shops spinning reel rigged with 6-pound-test high-vis Vicious line. He uses a Charlie Brewer Slider Grub on a 1/16-ounce, double-light wire jighead and a Lindy Balsawood float.

"I think this will work on any lake with plenty of baitfish and crappie. It's easy, and you don't need fancy electronics. Simply cast beyond the cover and bring the jig back to it. Once you reach the cover, stop the jig. Let it bump the cover. One thing I've found is that when you find a crappie in one part of a stake bed or brush pile, it's important to throw back to the exact spot. That's usually where all the fish will be holding."

He says the bite is subtle, but with no wind, it's easy to see. The bite is often a small movement down or to the side. The float usually doesn't go under.

This is a hit-or-miss situation, but when crappie move into shallow-water chasing food, they are relatively easy to catch.

Tip: If there were one ideal depth to catch fish, it would be 10 feet in waters that have a little stain. This strike zone is deep enough that fish aren't too spooky but not too deep to be difficult to fish. It can be jigged without adding too much weight to rigs. It's a good casting depth when fish are concentrated. Everything about the 10-foot range is just right: finding fish, controlling baits, setting depth and catching fish. However, it's up to the crappie when they are in the 10-foot zone.

NOTES

CHAPTER 31
Slow Trolling Mid-Depths & Deep Water

"Spider rigging, also called slow trolling, is definitely my bread-and-butter technique," says Dan Dannenmueller. "It's great in the winter, but it's a good technique all 12 months of the year."

Dannenmueller is an Alabama fisherman who, with his partner, was two-time Crappie Masters Angler Team of the Year, and he has competed in national tournaments from the north to far south. He and partner Garrett Steele were 2016 Alabama State Champion runner-ups in a prestigious event on the Crappie Masters trail. He has many sponsors and promotes them through social media, seminars and his work with journalists, writers, radio hosts and TV.

"If I could pick my ideal situation, it would be spider rigging in 12 to 16 feet of water. That's a good fishing depth where fish aren't too spooky but the depth is still an easy depth to fish. The actual depth of the crappie will depend upon many factors, including the lake or river being fished, water clarity, temperature and other factors. Winter means fish can be very deep in lakes. On the Alabama River the fish are often only eight to 12 feet even in winter. Move to a lake and they may be 20 feet or deeper.

"My primary poles are 14-foot BnM Duck Commander and 16-foot BnM BGJP jigging poles. These have a little backbone, but the main thing is the sensitivity of the tips. A sensitive pole is critical for seeing the light bites of winter. For pole length, getting baits further away from the boat means more bites. The shallower or clearer the water, the more important the length. There is a definite trade-off because the longer poles are more difficult to handle, control and use. If you are not familiar with using long poles, it's important to know that they can be a logistical nightmare if they all get tangled. So start out by limiting the number of poles you use, and stick to the shorter 12-foot models. As you gain experience, you can add more poles and move up in length.

"Winter slow trolling means very, very slow presentations. It almost means a dead stop, usually over brushpiles, stumps, logs and similar wood cover. We may start at 0.1 to 0.2 mph to work an area, ledge or cover. This will change based upon what we find and what the crappie want.

"Our setup for two people in front includes eight poles set an equal distance apart at the pole tip. They are set in individual pole holders made by Driftmaster. The holders are very important because they allow us maximum flexibility

to adjust poles. The long stems from the floor to the holder allow us to adjust them to where they are near our knees without being in the way.

"Electronics are essential for spider rigging. My preference is Garmin because they have moved into the lead on cutting-edge technology that relates into clearer images with more detail. The great definition can assist in picking and eliminating different spots. Since winter crappie are relating to cover, having better definition leads to better fishing because some spots can be ignored so time isn't wasted fishing them. Good spots can be pinpointed, making fishing time more productive. The GPS function is important for marking spots. And we use Side View religiously because we see more water per pass, again maximizing our time by finding more spots quicker and letting us zero in on them.

"In the winter, we will likely be positioned over ledges, brush, previous GPS points we've marked. Fish are often feeding on shad this time of year just as they do many of the other months. Crappie will always locate on cover, but if the cover has shad present, it will be much better. Other fish will be with the bait, feeding on schools of shad. This is especially true on a couple days of warming when the shad move up shallower, maybe as shallow as seven feet.

"In cold water, you seldom get the hard bites that pull the rod tips down. You'll get the subtle little bites, so seeing the line is very important," says Dannenmueller.

"Winter baits are typically downsized some from what are used in other seasons. We use a swivel at the end of our main line and then tie our bait rigs with a snap swivel. We use a mono or fluorocarbon line in 8-pound test. We like to use TTI Blakemore Mr. Crappie Tru-Turn hooks. We use the snelled, pre-tied hook in a #1 or #2 for the upper hook. The lower end can be another hook or a Road Runner or Bobby Garland Mo Glo head. The jig body will be a Bobby Garland and probably an Itty Bit Swim-R in the small 1.5-inch size.

The small jigs are perfect for spider rigging and tipping with a small minnow.

"It's funny to listen to fishermen discuss all the different colors they like to use. That's part of the fun of fishing. For us, we've had good luck with two shad-type colors called Glacier and Monkey Milk. They work great in most of the waters we fish. Blue ice is another good choice. A bold black-chartreuse color is the one that usually works if the shad colors do not."

Dannenmueller's Equipment List
- Ranger boat.
- Garmin electronics.
- Driftmaster rodholders.
- 14-foot BnM Duck Commander poles.
- 16-foot BnM BGJP poles.
- Mitchell spinning reels.
- Gamma 10-pound high-vis line.
- Tru-Turn #1 and #2 hooks.
- Heads: Road Runner, Garland Mo Glo.
- Jig body: Bobby Garland plastics.

Deep Water…Shallow Fish

"A good example of winter slow trolling," says Dannenmueller, "was a trip to Washington Lake in Mississippi. It was late winter, almost early spring, but on the particular day I remember, it was about 40 degrees with a drizzly rain and northwest wind. It felt really cold to us, but the water was a few degrees warmer.

"The crappie liked the low barometer as the front was approaching. The fish were out in 10 or 12 feet of water, but they were suspended up just under the surface. The mist provided a low-light condition that made a big difference. We slow trolled with our baits just under the surface, with our jigs at about 1.5 feet deep. The fish hammered them.

"Winter slow trolling can produce good fish whether they are in deep water or just up under the surface like they were at Washington. No matter what depth, the fish will still be relating to contours. At Washington, it was really important to be where the water dropped off into deeper water. We caught 40 crappie, including one at 2.75 pounds.

"So winter slow trolling is all about going slow, having baits at the right depth and watching for light bites."

Tips & Tricks

- "The advantage of spider rigging, even in the winter, is covering productive water effectively. There are multiple baits in the water so that's a big advantage," says Dannenmueller.
- "There will be line tangles when using long poles. If we get in a school of white bass and they tangle all the lines, we work out one pole at a time. We will

likely unclip the bait rig and put a new one on because it saves a lot of time."
- "The fish might be on a ledge or in holes. A brushpile in 20 feet that comes up to 10 feet is perfect in the winter. Fish will likely be positioned in the upper part of the brushpile, but depending upon the conditions, might be in deeper depths or on bottom. We always start looking for the shallow fish first. Our electronics will show us where the most crappie are located, but only by fishing will we know if those fish are active."
- "Bites are usually very light in the winter. It could be the line moving ever so slightly to one side or the tension coming off the rod tip. The fish might take the bait and not move.
- "You can find and catch fish with basic electronics. Advanced extras like Down Imaging, PanOptics and Side View change the overall level of fishing. You can see down, in front and to the side, making it quicker to find cover and fish."
- "A trick to hold a minnow on the hook, and at the same time entice more strikes, is to use a scent called Stubby Steve's. This rubbery, scent-filled product is made to produce strong, enticing scent, but it also helps keep a minnow from being easily knocked off a hook. That's a big advantage."

- "Change something. Our number-one problem as a team is staying too long in one area. A lot of times I think we spook the fish by staying too long or they get use to what we are doing. If this happens, we might change jig colors, depth or presentation speed. We change something to try and draw strikes and use electronics to see if fish are there or have moved. No matter what, we try not to take too long to make these changes. If they don't work, it's time to move.
- "Fishing isn't always easy. Picking the right spot, using the right bait and right presentation is important, but sometimes the fish just don't bite. You read about all the fish that experienced and pro fishermen catch. However, even though there are many good trips, there are plenty of days on the water when we struggle as much as anyone else. Don't get discouraged. Keep trying, know that others struggle, too, and never give up."
- "Logs, deadheads and other submerged covers help to position winter fish. Be sure to target high-percentage covers to put more fish in your boat during a day of fishing."
- "High-vis line is very important to me. It helps see more of the very-light winter bites. Not being able to see line can cost you many fish."

- "Here's a long-shot tip. When you are seeing fish on the locator but not getting a bite, try using a Crappie Rattle. Jam it up into a plastic jig, coat the jig with scent, maybe tip it with a very small minnow. Drop the bait to the fish. Jiggle and bounce it a little, then leave it alone. The noise might be something to trigger a few extra bites when the situation is right."
- "Being patient is a major advantage in the winter months. Slow down."
- "Fish good cover. A laydown in 20 feet of water coming up to 5 or 10 feet is an excellent spot for holding crappie. Don't pass these up, and be prepared to fish from the top of the cover all the way to the bottom."
- "Don't use fluoro line in the winter because it gets really stiff. My choice is high-vis Gamma."
- "Whether fishing in Alabama or Florida, when water is really cold, some of the big fish might bury up in the mud. I've had a diver tell me about seeing them, and we've caught fish with mud on their belly and fins. They are not actively feeding but can be caught by putting a bait in front of their noses."

Staying Warm

Dannenmueller says, "Being cold on the water isn't fun. We start out by layering. My bottom layers are by Cabela's and are their version of Under Armour. Next I prefer to have a heavyweight cotton shirt followed by a warm hoodie. My outside coat is by Stormr and is really warm. On bottom, I start with Cabela's under base, then flannel-lined jeans, followed with Stormr bibs.

"Hand warmers are very important. We use the common ones that can be shaken and placed in pockets. We can put our hands in our pockets and warm them, and our gloves. The warmth in the pockets also help us with our body heat. We also use good, warm insulated boots with thick socks and foot warmers similar to the hand warmers.

"Staying warm in cold weather is a matter of dressing right with warm clothing. You can't fish if you're too cold."

CHAPTER 32
Lake Drawdown

Winter is the time when Corps of Engineers flood-control lakes are brought down to lower levels to prepare for heavy spring rains. Some lakes are dropped a few feet, while others are dropped 15 feet or more. A drawdown basically creates a new lake with good fishing spots. The primary advantage of a lower lake level means more fish per acre. The disadvantages can include launch ramps out of the water and navigation problems.

Shallow Water: There are three depth zones to check when looking for drawdown crappie. One is in shallow water, similar to that in previous chapters. These are places where a few days of southern winds and sunshine warm shallow mudflats and coves. A warm-up of only a few degrees can cause baitfish to move into an area. Catching fish in a foot or two of water is not uncommon. Only by test-fishing spots will you learn when fish are in these areas. Northern spots in the afternoons are your best areas to try.

Mid-Depth Zone: The middle depths are easy to fish and can be great fish-catching areas in the winter. Although most fishermen think "deep water" in the winter, the fish in the upper layers will likely be more active and willing to take a bait. Key spots during winter drawdown are ledges with cover in 10 to 15 feet of water. This zone includes crappie that aren't too spooky, so a variety of fishing methods can be used. If fish are really stacked up in one location, an anchored boat is a big advantage because it lets you put your back to the wind and get lower in the boat to say warm.

Deep: Deep-water areas give crappie a comfortable temperature zone, places to hide from predators and a food supply. Therefore, deep water often has everything they need. What's deep? Every body of water is different, but in a stained lake, it's usually everything below 15 feet. In a clear lake, deep water may be considered 40 feet or deeper. The greatest deep-water advantage is fish are more stable even when a front passes. Good cover and deep water can produce some outstanding catches.

Scouting: Drawdown situations are perfect times to scout. A contour map and GPS unit allows you to mark spots you can't see during normal water conditions. For example, with the lake down five feet, you see two stumps side by side about one foot under the water. Your locator indicates a four-foot depth. Therefore, at normal pool, these stumps will be in nine feet of water with the top of the stumps at six feet, making them perfect for spring and fall.

You'll also find small feeder ditches running into the lake, rockslide areas, logs and other structures that can help you catch more fish when water is at normal pool. A little work during the drawdown period is worth many bonus fish later.

NOTES

CHAPTER 33
Factors & Tips – Winter

- Wind. A lot of wind is bad, but a little wind is an advantage because the ripples on top of the water make crappie less spooky and more willing to bite. The chop also oxygenates the water. Wind adds a factor of wind chill, so dress appropriately.
- Cold Front. Fronts during any season changes barometric pressure and can cause crappie to become negative feeders. Shallow-water fish are more sensitive to fronts than deeper ones.
- Rain/Clouds. Less sun will usually allow fish to move further away from cover, causing them to be scattered and harder to find. Winter is one time they may stay on cover no matter the conditions and light penetration.
- Fishing Pressure. Spring is the busiest time of year because it's "crappie season". Winter is becoming more popular, but there will still be fewer fishermen on the lake than in the spring because many won't brave the cold temperatures.

Question: What's more important when you're getting super-light bites…feel or watching line?

- Charles Bunting says, "Watching your line is more important. Sometimes the bite will be so light you won't feel it. If a fish just mouths the bait, you won't see it on your rod tip or feel it, but you can see the little twitch in the line. Normally, the bigger the fish the lighter the bite. A trick when slow trolling is to use high-visibility line."
- "Feel is important," says Barry Morrow. "Most of my fishing is with a pole in my hand. I hold the pole light, like squeezing a bird without hurting it. The key for good "feel" when vertical jigging is to use a heavy jig like a 1/8-ounce or 1/4-ounce. The heavy jig is very important to keep the line tight."
- Phil Rambo says, "When I'm long-line trolling, I'll change techniques if the bites are light because we're not going to catch the fish. We will slow troll and watch our rod tips. If bites are really light, I will probably put poles in the holder but hold one in my hand so I can feel it. When I'm holding a pole, I'll place my index finger on the line to help feel the bites."

Other tips from fishermen:

- When vertical jigging, you've got to watch the line or you're missing bites. High-vis line is critical.

- I think a pole holder is an advantage during light bites because the poles are held still so it's easier to see the line move.
- I use a heavy jig, so I'm guessing I'll see five percent of my bites and feel 95 percent. My jigs are 1/8- or 1/4-ounce, so it keeps the line tight and I'll feel more bites. Watching line is more important with a lighter jig because of the percentage of bites you see instead of feel. Concentration is important, too. If you're watching birds you're missing bites.

Question: How important is being quiet in the boat?

- "We're pretty quiet," says Toni Collins. "I think banging stuff around in the boat can spook fish. We're usually focused upon poles and lines, so being quiet usually isn't a problem."
- "Being quiet is very important," says Jim Duckworth. "I turn locators off. Use one speed and keep it constant. Wind can be used for your advantage to move quietly. I use a Power Pole in the wind, both to anchor and to raise and lower a wind sock."
- Todd Huckabee says, "There are situations when it's important to be quiet like in very shallow, clear water, but I've guided many trips when we were laughing, talking and the clients are jumping around and slamming lids or dropping stuff and we still catch fish. In

general, it's not too important. Another example is at Truman Lake. A team like Charlie and Kevin Rogers will bust into a cove, motor almost to the tree they are going to fish and plop the trolling motor down and get to the tree and catch fish. Most teams are aggressive and not too quiet, yet they catch a lot of crappie."

- "It's very important to be quiet when you're in 10 feet of water or less," says Brad Whitehead. "In deeper water, the fish are not as spooky and are use to boat traffic."

Other be-quiet tips from fishermen:

- Being quiet is important if you're fishing from a single-wall aluminum boat but not too critical from a triple-wall glass boat.
- It's very important to be quiet in an aluminum boat. The noise will spook fish.
- Just like your daddy told you when you were a kid, "Sit down and shut up…you're going to scare off the fish." I've played the radio and caught fish, but I believe your bigger fish got that way for a reason, and you'll more likely catch one if you're quiet.
- Being quiet is important in shallow-water. It's a big advantage to be fishing out of a fiberglass boat.

Favorite Colors

These are color choices given by different fishermen.

- In plastic, it would be chartreuse/white, black, and in mylar, it's a purple/blue tint.
- Glow lemon/lime, black/chartreuse and red/white.
- Popsicle, silver smoke and black/silver.
- Three colors to take to any lake are white/chartreuse, black/chartreuse and red/chartreuse.
- Black/chartreuse; pink/charteuse in muddy water; blue/chartreuse in clear.
- Electric chicken, blue/white, black/chartreuse.
- Orange head with the following bodies: clear firecracker sparkle, red/chartreuse sparkle, black/chartreuse sparkle.
- Lime/chartreuse, blue/chartreuse, yellow/white.
- White/chartreuse, chartreuse multicolor, junebug/chartreuse.

Winter Safety

A fall into the lake can be fatal in winter. I like to carry a simple, basic survival bag. It includes several hand warmers, a towel, an old pair of coveralls, socks, toboggan and gloves. The theory is to remove wet clothes, dry off with the towel and put on dry clothes to survive until you get back to the ramp or get help. This is not high-tech but is economical and could save your life.

CHAPTER 34
Caring for Your Catch

Except for eating, the fun stops when you catch a crappie. However, proper care of the fish is important to taste, and is an ethical obligation. The following are tips for "After the Catch" whether you keep the fish for eating or release it.

After the Catch – Putting Crappie On Ice

Want a mess of crappie to eat? There are two recommended methods: livewell or ice. Healthy fish can go directly into the livewell. Keep them alive until cleaning.

Throwing fish on ice guarantees all fish will be in good condition for cleaning when you arrive home. There are two important keys for using ice. The first one is to use plenty of ice to quickly and completely cool the fish. The second rule is the most critical…don't keep dead fish in water. Be sure to keep all water drained from your cooler. Water, even ice-cold water, will cause quick deterioration of the fish.

Tip: I have a friend who often transfers fish from his livewell into a spare freezer when he gets home. He says the meat is always firm, making it easier to fillet. This also works great if you don't have time to clean fish when you get home.

Mounting a Trophy

A good mount begins with treating the fish like you have a trophy. Handle it gently. Letting the fish flop around in the net or on the floor of the boat can knock scales off and cause other damage.

Keep it alive in the livewell or put it on ice. Don't let it die and stay in water.

Get it into the freezer as soon as possible. You can protect the fins by wrapping it in a damp towel, but the key is to wrap it tightly in a plastic bag so it won't freezer burn. Repeat, don't let it freezer burn!

Select a good taxidermist.

Livewells

Maximizing livewell use comes from knowledge and many good and bad experiences. Serious tournament fishermen are, in general, the most knowledgeable because they fish in all conditions, temperatures and types of water, and they have money riding on each decision they make. I've noticed two items in most serious tournament boats in the summer: bottles of ice and oxygen.

The first segment tips are taken from various sources. The last comments are from tournament fishermen. Both segments lead to the fact that keeping fish, or bait, alive in a livewell does not require being a rocket scientist, but the success or failure is due to scientific factors, including oxygen and contaminants. Oxygen levels must be kept up, and negative factors like ammonia must be kept to tolerable levels.

Cleaning Your Livewell

Phil Rambo says, "We clean our livewell after every trip. We're usually at a campground, so we'll just use a hose and flush it out. We'll remove the screen and clean it. Then, we'll flush the livewell out some more with the screen in. We found by cleaning it every time our fish are healthier and will stay alive much better. We also clean our minnow tank by moving our minnows over, cleaning the tank and putting fresh water in it. We clean everything with clean water, no detergents or cleaning agents. The water may have a little chlorine in it, but by letting it dry overnight and adding another 50 gallons of fresh lake water to our livewell the next day, it's not a problem. We use Keep Alive chemical in the minnows and Please Release Me in our livewell."

Mike Parrott says, "I rinse my livewell out, then take a shop-vac and vacuum it out. I sometimes fill it with clean water and let it circulate to clean the hoses. Then I leave the lid open and let the sun dry it. I think that probably kills anything bad that is left in it."

Livewell Notes from the Pros

- Oxygen levels are inversely proportional to rising water temperatures the number of fish per unit of water and contaminants in the water.
- Rising water temperatures can be controlled by adding ice to the livewell. It is recommended to lower well water temperatures 10-12 degrees below the lake temperature. This will help improve oxygen levels, yet won't shock the fish.
- Maintain a reasonable number of fish per unit of water. Experience may be the best teacher. Also, as water temperature rises, fewer fish can be maintained.
- Change at least half of the water in the livewell every three or four hours to reduce ammonia buildup.
- Add non-iodized salt or other "Catch and Release" chemicals. Salt formula is one cup of salt for every 15 gallons of water.
- Fact: Several fish can be kept alive in a small livewell if it is kept aerated/oxygenated. Oxygen introduced will increase the numbers allowed in a fixed area.
- Fill livewells as soon as the boat is launched. Turn on the recirculating aerator immediately to begin building oxygen levels, and run it continuously all day.
- Water frozen in plastic bottles will lower temperatures and keep the chlorine out of the tank.

- Turn on the livewell when away from the launch ramp. There may be oil and gas in the water at the ramp. Turn it on early and add ice to drop the temperature when it's hot.
- A fishing guide may need to keep 100 fish in a livewell. Seldom will the fish die if you keep the livewell on "fill" or "auto." The flowing water supplies oxygen and removes the nitrates that kill fish. The only negative is the humming noise.
- Use a good aerator. Install the bubbler in the back of the boat to minimize noise, and then run air lines to your livewell. Add a five-inch disc stone to each line to give more bubbles.

Releasing Fish

There are fish you'll catch that you want to release. Most are small ones. Others may come after you have a limit. Many serious crappie fishermen will release their huge fish to help keep good genes in the species. No matter the reason, good release habits are important so the fish can be reproductive and be caught again.

Important for Crappie

- Never pull on the fishing line to free a hook from a fish. It won't work and will further damage the fish. Grab the hook with your fingers or pliers and push it out backwards until the barb clears.

- Handle the crappie as little as possible. The slime coating protects the skin. Removing it can cause the fish to be sick later.
- If you catch a huge crappie that is badly hooked, try cutting the hook off near the barb so you can push the hook back out without hurting the big slab.
- There are two distinct thoughts on badly hooked crappie but, before trying them, consider keeping any fish you don't think will live. (1) A popular method used by many fishermen and one supported by the Missouri Department of Conservation is the cut the line. The flesh around the hook will die back and the hook will fall out. (2) Some say that hooks in fish don't quickly fall out. This group recommends taking as much care as possible and remove the hook. My recommendation is to keep any seriously injured fish. If you eat it, you know it will not be wasted. If you release the fish, first cut the line. I don't know the mortality, but it will do less immediate damage to the fish and you can get it back into the water quickly.
- In summer, fish caught in deep water will usually die. You can puncture and "fizz" the fish to release the pressure from the air bladder so the fish can upright itself in the water. Sometimes it works, and sometimes it doesn't.

General Release Tips

- Any really big crappie, bass or other big fish you catch has the best chance for survival if you keep the fish in the water. However, this is not practiced by any crappie fisherman I've been with or watched.
- Flatten hook barbs by pinching them with pliers. This makes hook removal very simple. However, because we are often catching fish to eat or maybe for a tournament, we usually don't fish with a barbless hook.
- Make life easier on yourself (and the fish) by always using pliers.

Fizzing a Crappie

"You stick a fish to release air from an air bladder," says Ronnie Capps. "When a fish is upright in the livewell, his gills are working, but when he's on his side, one of his gills is not working. His mouth is chomping."

Capps says the problem is mainly a depth situation, with 18 to 25 feet or deeper being the common range when the problem occurs. Also, warmer water situations make the problem more difficult. You can tell when a crappie is in trouble by the way they act and when they start popping their mouth.

"The easiest way to stick, also called fizzing, is to use the BnM Measurer," says Capps. "The measurer stops the flopping and allows you to line the fish up just right. It also shows the exact spot to stick the fish. Insert the needle at a 45-degree angle under a scale. After you go under the scale, turn the needle up to a 90-degree angle and go straight into the fish's air bladder. Go about half way through the fish and, in ten seconds, it should be normalized. If you've done a good job, it will go to the bottom of the livewell."

CHAPTER 35
Cleaning

A Good Cleaning Station

Nothing can break your back more quickly than bending over cleaning a big bunch of crappie. If you clean fish often, there's no reason not to have a good setup. The following are some ideas for things you might want in a station.

First, have a cleaning table at the right height. Make it where you won't be bending over to clean fish. Experiment to learn the best height for you or maybe make it adjustable.

Two, have everything within reach when you, begin cleaning. Pans, knives and other accessories should be handy. Make special holders or storage areas for each item.

Three, have water and electricity nearby. Make sure you follow good safety practices because electricity and water isn't a good combination.

Four. A sink to clean the fish is good. An old sink can be built into the station.

Jim Duckworth has a practical cleaning station. He placed a 5-amp solar panel on the roof with a line down to a battery so it stays fully charged all the time. The battery, located in an aluminum box, has 12-volt hookups for electric knives and lighting.

"My station includes a stainless-steel sink with sprayer. I just hook a hose up to it whenever I'm cleaning fish. I have a piece of Plexiglas cut to the exact width of my table, and it's set up so the water runs off to the outside edge. I also have a hole in the countertop with a plastic bag for guts and waste.

"With a roof overhead, I can clean fish if it's raining, sunny or dark. I recommend a good cleaning station for any fishermen who cleans fish. It's just so much easier."

Pan-Dressing

Tools needed: fillet knife, spoon or scaling tool, cutting board, bucket for waste, bowl of water for dressed fish, paper towels.

Why pan-dress? The first reason is to waste less meat. Filleting will cause some of the meat to be lost. The second reason is that pan-dressing fish leaves the tail, skin and bones. Many people say the meat has a better taste when cooked with the bones.

You can separate the meat from the bones while eating. The fried tail, often called a potato chip, is a crunchy, crispy treat.

Steps for Cleaning

- Use a tablespoon or scaling tool to remove all the scales. Scrape from the tail to the head until the skin is smooth and scale-free.
- Use a sharp knife to remove the head. Also, take off the pectoral fins.
- Use the knife to open the belly and remove all entrails.
- Rinse in clean water several minutes to clean out all blood and oils.

Filleting

Tools needed: electric fillet knife; small fillet knife; cutting board; bucket for waste; bowl of water for fillets; paper towels.

When you fillet a crappie, you'll lose a little meat from along the backbone, ribs and collar. I agree that a pan-cleaned fish has a little better taste and more meat, but you'll find every piece of fish in my freezer filleted because I hate eating around bones and risking a bone in my throat. There is nothing more enjoyable than sinking my teeth into a piece of filleted crappie.

Steps for Cleaning

1. Lay the fish on the cutting board with the back facing you. Hold the fish by the mouth. Place the electric fillet knife just behind the pectoral (side)

fin. Cut downward to the backbone, but be careful not to cut into the backbone.
2. Turn the knife blade toward the tail and continue cutting. You'll feel resistance as you cut through the rib cage. Get all the meat possible, but do not cut through the backbone. Continue toward the tail until you get within one-quarter or one-eighth inch of the tail.
3. The fillet is barely attached to the tail. Flip it away from the fish, and position your knife on the narrow portion of the fillet. While holding the fish, slice between the meat and skin to remove the fillet. Place the fillet, with rib cage still attached, to the side. Flip the fish over and fillet the other side.
4. Take the fillets and carefully cut out the rib cage with the tip of your knife. To keep the most meat, angle the knife to cut close to the ribs.
5. Rinse the fillets until you remove all waste and oils.

Option I: At step 3, most fishermen will flip the fish over and cut with the belly facing them on the second cut. If you keep the back toward you, it's possible to get more meat. It may be very awkward until you become use to it.

Option II: At step 4, pick up the finished fillet by the rib bones and cut the ribs off with the electric fillet knife. You save the full step of cutting out the ribs.

Option III: At step 4, use a pair of scissors to cut the rib bones from the fillet.

Cleaning Tip: Phil Rambo says to keep the smell from getting bad in the trashcan, you can put the remains in a plastic bag and place them in the freezer. Pull them out of the freezer on trash day or when you haul your trash away. No bad smell or problems with dogs in the trashcan.

Tool Notes
- A sharp, short fillet knife makes removing the ribs easier.
- A tablespoon or scaling tool is used to take off scales.
- The cutting board can be almost any material, but a plastic or Plexiglas board is easier to clean and handle.
- Paper towels are important to keep everything clean.
- A clean knife and board result in cleaner, better-tasting meat.

Motel Cleaning: You can use the top of your cooler or the tailgate of a truck (preferably your fishing partner's truck) to clean fish. You'll need a cutting board if using the tailgate. Cleaning fish at a motel may be okay if you are having a fish fry, but don't routinely do this because a bloody, stinking parking lot won't leave a good impression of crappie fishermen to others staying at the motel.

Fish Scalers: There are mechanical scalers available to save you the time and trouble of physically removing the scales. One version is pulled behind the boat. It rotates and knocks the scales off. Another model is for use on shore. It has a motor, drum and uses water to clean the scales. If you scale your fish and leave the skin on, it can save you cleaning time.

Electric Fillet Knife: A 12-volt knife allows you to clean fish at a boat or vehicle. Some prefer it for safety; no deadly 110-volt AC. Maybe the most important factor for selecting your knife is feel. You need a comfortable knife that fits your hands.

Properly Store Fish

You go to the trouble of cleaning a mess of crappie, so you want them to be in excellent condition when you get ready to fry them. Fishermen unanimously agree that the best tasting fish are those fried fresh immediately after cleaning. However, there's nothing like having a backup supply in the freezer, so here's what the pros say.

- Fresh fish taste best.
- A key to good-tasting fish is to wash them after cleaning and rewash them until they are clean and all of the oils are removed.
- Freeze in water. This is highly recommended over vacuum packing by some of the fishermen.

- Store in quart bags with 10 to 15 fillets per bag. Add water. Squeeze out the air. Seal.
- Cut the top out of a milk carton, place fish to within two inches of the top, then add water until there is one inch of water over the fillets.
- Vacuum sealing is recommended over water by some fishermen. The advantages include less weight and storage space, good freezer life and you have quicker thawing.
- Taking care of your fish means a good-tasting meal. Take your time and do it right.
- Question: Why is it called "dressing" a fish when we are undressing it?

NOTES

CHAPTER 36
Cooking

Frying Fish

You can poach, broil, bake and smoke crappie, but none of them match the taste of fried fish. If frying has a downfall, it's the fact that too much fried foods are bad for us. However until the doctor says otherwise, give me fried crappie.

- Keep grease around 350 degrees.
- Clean grease gives the best-tasting results.
- Never cover cooked fish with a lid or they'll get soggy.
- Place something in the bottom of the pan where you put the fried crappie to soak up excess grease.

Frying Tips

Larry Whiteley, former Manager of Communications for Bass Pro Shops, has fried fish for thousands of people over the years. He says, "I use a 'Better Breader' container where the fillets go in the top and the breading in the bottom. By tilting and shaking, the breading goes on the fillets evenly. It's important to have all the fish covered in breading. I use Uncle Bucks original or spicy. I drop the fillet in the oil, usually peanut oil, that's been heated to 325 to 350 degrees. When the fish floats to the top, it's done. It's difficult to keep fillets hot and crispy when cooking for a lot of people, so it's best if they eat it as it comes out. It's funny because there is something about frying fish that people love to watch. And they like to talk about it and try samples. I've cooked on every type fryer, but the Cajun Fryer with multiple baskets allows cooking more than just fish at the same time. For example, I can put fish in one basket and fries in the other. With temperature being a key factor, the Cajun Fryer is the best I've used. It's important to keep the grease hot and get a good, quick seal so the fillets are encased and therefore don't soak up the grease while cooking."

Steve "Bruno" Perotti says, "I use Andy's breading, clean grease and use a Cajun Fryer. I cook the fish until they float and take them out. I place them in a roaster pan with the bottom lined with bread to soak up the grease."

Other fishermen commented:

- The best-tasting fish comes from a cast-iron skillet with about one inch of grease in it. It's just a better taste.
- I cook at 350 degrees with a Cajun Fryer. When the fish floats, I cook it for one more minute because I

- prefer them crispy. Never put a solid lid on them or they will steam and turn to mush.
- I still like vegetable oil and "cornmeal mix". When they are brown, they're ready.
- It takes a lot of paper towels, maybe 10 layers on bottom, but they're important to keep fish from getting mushy. The towels act like a wick to soak up grease.
- Don't cover the fish with a lid or it will steam them.
- I use an RV Cajun Fryer at 350 degrees. The fryer allows you to use the grease over and over again. I use Bass Pro Shops Cottonseed Oil because it has a higher flash point.
- If your grease needs cleaning, run a batch or two of sliced potatoes. It helps.
- For years I used half corn meal, half pancake mix, salt, pepper, and small amount of paprika. Today, I like prepared types, including JR Mad and Drakes Batter Mix.

Air Fryer

Fast forward to 2018. A great product making headlines is the air fryer. Remove 80% of the grease, fats and calories and you have a healthier fillet to eat. The remarkable thing about the fish is they taste fried. There may be a small difference to expert fish eaters, but the difference is so small it's barely noticeable. Potato fries are outstanding. Plus the fryer can be used for almost anything you normally fry in grease.

If for nothing else but better health, the air fryer is worth the money. However, another advantage is time. Fish can be cooked in less time than it takes to get the grease into a fryer and heated up. Plus, no grease has to be bought.

The downside of a fryer is size. It takes up space on a counter, and the amount of fish it can cook at one time is small. So a fryer is best for one to four people.

Final review: Personally, I only enjoy fish that is fried; not microwaved, baked or otherwise prepared. I give the air fryer an A+ because foods taste like fried foods while prolonging the clogged arteries for a few more years.

Top Fixin's

French fries; fried potatoes; potato-chip-style deep-fried potatoes; white beans; fried banana pepper dipped in fish batter; fried okra; hushpuppies; coleslaw.

Next to catching crappie, two things rank high on the list of fun things to do. One is to talk about catching crappie, and the other is eating them.

CHAPTER 37
The "Difference Makers" in Crappie Fishing

There are special people who have made a difference in our sport. For example, husband-wife teams Phil and Eva Rambo and Don and Toni Collins, and others, are respected as great sportsmen and ambassadors of crappie fishing. Jimmy Houston and Bill Dance were good for crappie fishing in earlier years because of their personalities and television exposure. Jim Duckworth instructed through seminars, magazine articles and fishing videos. Steve McCadams has been a guide and outdoor writer for decades. Many fishermen I consider old-timers who have been good for the sport are people I respect. Not all who deserve special mention can be included in this chapter, but the ones you'll read about have contributed something special to the sport. I call them the "Difference Makers."

Industry Pioneer...Buck Simmons

"Buck Simmons recently received the Lifetime Achievement Award from Crappie Masters and was inducted to the Legends of the Outdoors Hall of Fame. Buck has designed, improved and made cutting-edge fishing poles for many decades. His BGJP pole, Buck's Graphite Jig Pole, forever changed crappie fishing. He has made our fishing more efficient, enjoyable, and has always supported crappie magazines and tournaments. If you have held a long pole for crappie or bluegill fishing, it was developed by, or at least influenced by, Buck Simmons."

…Tim Huffman

Wilson "Buck" Simmons, long-time owner of BnM Pole Company, started working after school in the summer when he was 12 years old. He went to Mississippi State and spent two years in Turkey while serving in the Army, then returned to work.

The BnM story? Simmons says, "It started as the Broom and Mop Company. We had broken broom handles we couldn't use, and somebody suggested we attach them to bamboo poles for bream fishing. We retailed them for $1.50, and that was a lot of money back then. In about 1957, we started making jointed poles. Our next pole was our first fiberglass called the Little Jewel for bream. Next came the Cadillac that was a fiberglass telescopic for crappie. That pole was a big seller because at that time it was the lightest pole available.

"Jigging was getting really big in Arkansas, and those fishermen wanted something lighter they could fish with all

day long. We made one stiffer than a fly rod and with eyes. Once the word got out, we started selling them. We called it our Buck's Graphite Jigging Pole."

Business strength? "From day one, we had inventory. Some companies don't. I always took pride in that."

Other comments about your career? "I really had fun. I traveled with business friends. I got to fish a lot especially when travelling. Fishing at home was usually work because I was trying to improve the poles."

Any advice? "It's simple. Live by the golden rule. Do unto others as you would have them do unto you."

Buck was born in 1937. His fishing hero is a friend named Cotton. American heroes are Ronald Regan and John Wayne. His favorite food is fried chicken. Sport team, Mississippi State basketball. Favorite hobbies include his dogs, goats and horses. Pet peeve: liars. Biggest crappie, several over three pounds.

How would you like to be remembered? "As being the man who developed the best product that improved the way people catch crappie."

Undisputed Champions of Crappie Fishing… Ronnie Capps & Steve Coleman

> "Ronnie and Steve are in this book for one simple reason—they are the best crappie-fishing team in the world. They are walking encyclopedias of crappie-fishing

knowledge and are willing to share it. They prove year after year they are great fishermen." ...Tim Huffman

Capps-Coleman credentials include over $1,750,000 in tournament winnings. Seven or eight National Championships with wins in Crappie USA, CAST and NACA. They recently won the American Crappie Trail 2017 Kentucky/Barkley tournament and were National Points Champions. They were inducted into the Legends of the Outdoors Hall of Fame in 2011. Both fishermen guide part-time.

Ronnie says, "Steve and I started fishing together as kids on Reelfoot Lake. We had cane poles and cat-gut line. Our minnow rigs were compact and tied out of 50-pound-test line. We had 12 feet of line on the pole, so that's the deepest we fished."

Steve agrees, "We would wind the line up on the tip of the pole, and then wind it up the pole toward the handle. If we broke the pole due to a big fish, we could still get it in with the line."

The team started by fishing bass tournaments and did okay but was embarrassed to fish with all the bass guys in nice boats. They fished their first crappie tournament in 1978 and went on to finish thirteenth in the classic that year. "We got whipped on the first day," says Ronnie. "We had never fished water so clear. That night we bought some two-pound test line for our cane poles and made a comeback." Their crappie heroes back then were Alan Padgett and Bobby Martin.

The team works very hard. They've placed cover in many lakes. During early tournaments when no pole limits existed, they would fish up to 24 long poles, not an easy chore. They've filled their boat with water so it would be more stable in the wind. They've been on the lake at 2:30 in the morning running Side Imaging looking for potential fishing spots.

Ronnie Capps was born in 1966 and is a Tennessee Wildlife Officer. His favorite food is anything quick, like hot wings; favorite show, Gunsmoke; and favorite all-time fisherman, Rick Clunn. A major influence was his Grandpa Parker. Something people may not know is that Ronnie is a certified diver and was an All-American college football player.

Biggest crappie: 3.69 pounds out of a canoe. Favorite lake is Pickwick. He says going all-out when they go fishing is just who they are.

Known for? Ronnie says, "I hope it's for fishing off the front of the boat. When we started fishing side by side, people thought we were crazy. It was two seats up front and controlling the boat with precision. I think we've helped a lot of people learn a technique they can use any season, deep or shallow."

Advice? "You can't make yourself do it. You have to love it whether it's fishing, trap shooting or whatever. If you don't love it, then it won't work for you."

Ronnie, when it's all over how would you like to be remembered? "For the hard work we did to catch fish. We don't have magic. We worked hard to earn what we've earned."

Steve Coleman was born 1963 and worked for the Department of Corrections. His favorite food is home-cooked roast beef; favorite movies, anything with John Wayne. His favorite lake is Grenada for big crappie and Reelfoot for numbers. Something people may not know is that Steve is a certified diver, and one of his hobbies is metal detecting water areas like docks and ramps.

"Diving has helped me learn about the bottom, how the drops were situated, how the roots of the old stumps were really shaped and where the fish would be holding. Ronnie and I walked around a lot on bottom. We learned about light. All of these things have helped visualize what's on bottom when we fish."

Advice? Steve says, "If you're going to be good at something, you have to have a burn, a fire for what you love and what you want to do."

When it's over how would you like to be remembered? "Honest."

Tournament Promoter & 1st Major Classic Champion...Paul Alpers

"Many people aren't aware that Paul fished in six classics, winning the first major classic. More recently, he won the 2017 Crappie Masters National Championship. As a tournament promoter, he transformed tournaments to a pay level never before reached. Thanks to Paul, we have nationally sponsored teams and tournaments paying more than they previously paid."…Tim Huffman

Paul Alpers has been in the poultry business, was a beer salesman and built missile silos. The past couple of decades, he worked in tournament promotions. He is proud he changed competitive crappie fishing by creating higher-paying tournaments.

How did you get into promotions? "I had been around tournaments for years. Several of us got together in 1995 when we learned Crappiethon was ending. We formed Crappie USA so national crappie tournaments wouldn't come to an end. Everyone in the group did something to make it work. My job was selling advertisements. After seven years, I changed jobs to help Crappie Masters get started so fishermen could compete for money they deserve."

Have tournament competitions changed? "A few good teams use to dominate. Ronnie Capps and Steve Coleman are examples. They are still great, but today there are many more good teams."

Fishing highlight? "It was all the time Dad spent fishing with me. We had a lot of good, quality time together. He taught me about fishing and life."

Paul's home water is Truman. Fishing hero is Bill Dance because he is a good role model. American heroes are cowboys like Roy Rogers and John Wayne. Favorite teams, KC Royals and Chiefs; favorite food, frog legs; hobbies, fishing, elk hunting; biggest crappie, 3.32 from Grenada.

How would you like to be remembered? "I hope people respect me for the hard work and time I put into Crappie Masters and that I helped make a difference in our sport. And, that I wasn't a bad crappie fisherman."

Tournament Director…Darrell Van Vactor

> "Darrell started guiding when he was 18 years old to help support going to college. Almost five decades later, he still guides part time but is better known for his contributions to tournament fishing. He opened the door for many fishermen with a grass-roots tournament trail and continues today as Crappie USA's General Manager."…Tim Huffman

Thirty-four years is a long time in the crappie-tournament business. He started with Crappiethon USA in 1984. He was one of the founders of Crappie USA in 1995 after Johnson Outdoors ended Crappiethon. "We wanted tournaments to continue," says Van Vactor. "A group of us got together and created the one- and two-day tournaments. It's been a great ride for me."

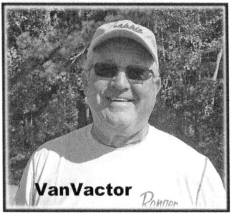

Changes? "A potential sponsor years ago told me, 'Oh yeah, the crappie fisherman is the guy sitting on the bank on a bucket with a pack of cigarettes rolled up in his sleeve, pack of beer beside him and staying all day even if he doesn't get a bite.' Back when we started few companies recognized crappie fishermen as major players in tournament fishing. Today most companies have crappie-specific products, giving fishermen much better equipment and tools, including great poles, line and accessories.

"Our first classic had one Ranger boat, and it was mine. The next classic, we had 16 and, since then, it's been about 60% at our tournaments. I'm very proud to have been a part of tournaments and promotions that helped improve the sport of crappie fishing and be a part of a long-term, grassroots tournament trail for our fishermen."

Crappie USA is the oldest national crappie circuit. What are you most proud of? "That's easy. We've donated over $334,000 in college scholarships. Along with that, it's all the many wonderful friends including press, sponsors and fishermen."

Technique Pioneer-Innovator...Roger Gant

"Few people have taken a new fishing technique and become famous for it. Roger has also been responsible for a technique-specific boat and pole. His side-pulling method is unique because the boat is kept sideways while fishing. It gives everyone in the boat an equal chance to catch fish. In addition, Roger and his brother Bill are nice, respected, Christian men." ...Tim Huffman

Roger Gant is owner of Pro Guide Service at Pickwick Lake. He was born in 1946. He and brother Bill won the 2011 Crappie Masters Classic and finished fifth in 2012. He has won tournaments on Pickwick, Ross Barnett, Grenada and Arklabutla.

His fishing hero is Bill Dance; American hero, Ronald Regan; favorite food, crappie; sport teams, St. Louis and Atlanta baseball; hobbies, enjoys deer hunting more than fishing; pet peeve, most politicians; biggest crappie, 3.25 on a cane pole at Pickwick.

Talk about your technique. "Side pulling came along about the same time as the first LCD graphs, and it opened up a whole new way of fishing in open-water. We moved from the bank to deep, open water.

"It lets us cover a lot of area by drifting or using the trolling motor to move. The trolling path is wide since the boat is sideways. Not only is it more fun, but you miss fewer fish. The baits are in the water 100 percent of the time. The wind blowing is not a problem."

He says the most different thing about the technique is that the trolling motor is close to the back fisherman and mounted on the side of the boat. Its advantage over forward trolling is that hooks are set on every bite and everyone in the boat has an equal chance to catch fish.

Strength and weakness? "I can go to a lake I don't know anything about and I'm able to catch fish. My weakness is shallow-water fishing."

Advice about life? "I think people taking time to do what they really enjoy is good for them."

How would you like to be remembered? "As someone who was pretty good at a fishing technique, had fun doing it and did it my way."

Guide & Teacher...Sam Heaton

"I remember listening to Sam giving seminars in Springfield, Missouri, when there was only one Bass Pro Shops store in the country. His seminars gave a platform for teaching crappie fishing while his 25 years of guiding on Weiss gave him one-on-one teaching time. He has always been comfortable in front of a crowd and enjoys entertaining while instructing. He one of a kind, a great promoter and a man with a big heart." ...Tim Huffman

Sam Heaton was born in 1949 and resides in Florida. His credentials include guiding, promotions, seminars, working for Spiderwire and Crappiethon USA. He worked for years as the Field Promotions Manager for Johnson Outdoors. He currently works with the American Crappie Trail.

Sam grew up in rural Alabama where the outdoors was a way of life. His love of the outdoors helped put fish and meat on the table. He served in the Army with the 75th Airborne

Ranger Battalion in Vietnam. He got wounded a few times but never seriously.

"I still love to crappie fish, but with Johnson, I was responsible for saltwater, so I spent a lot of time there, too. My favorite way to crappie fish now is fishing vertical structure. I've always been associated with BnM and have my own signature jig pole I like to use. I fish right down beside the bullrushes, canes and other vegetation here in Florida. It's fun and productive. I've always been a crappie fisherman at heart. It's the only sport where an 80-year-old man, nine-year-old girl, and seven-year-old boy can go fishing and all have the same expectations. It's great."

Sam's fishing heroes are Roland Martin, Curt Gouty, Ernest Hemingway and his mother. American heroes are military men and women. Favorite food: sweets. Favorite movies: Jeremiah Johnson and The Legend of Tom Horn. Book: Bleachers. Hobbies: waterfowl hunting, fishing, reading, walking in the Everglades. Biggest crappie, 3-lb 6-oz from Yellow Creek in 1996 from a dock while using a 1/16-ounce black/chartreuse tube jig.

Biggest strength? "Ability to read people. I'm comfortable with people, especially in a boat."

Are you still motivated? "I wish I were fishing right now instead of doing this interview with you."

How would you like to be remembered? "As a conservationist and outdoorsman."

Crappie-Fishing Superstore…Louie Mansfield

> "The Grizzly Jig store is without a doubt the best crappie fishing store in the country. Not only do they have tremendous inventory, the staff are crappie fishermen who can answer any question a customer might ask. They can also give you crappie-fishing tips. Their annual store sale and event is the weekend before the SuperBowl each year and is four days packed with free seminars from the best crappie fishermen in the country. Owner Louie Mansfield has created a crappie superstore." … Tim Huffman

Grizzly founder and owner Louie Mansfield is a good crappie fisherman and expert on Reelfoot Lake. He happiest with a jigging pole in his hand but spends most of his hours at the store.

Along with fishing tournaments for years, Louie and Grizzly Jig Company have always supported crappie tournaments and the sport of crappie fishing. He is one of the "good guys" in the industry.

For those wondering, the Grizzly Jig name comes from the jigs tied with the grizzly feathers from a duck. The Grizzly Jig store came about because Louie's job at the shipyard faded away. He had started selling jigs, tied by sons Wade and Lance, then made the jump to opening a store. Like the popular saying, "The rest is history."

"Mr. Crappie"…Wally Marshall

"Wally Marshall can thank Bass Pro Shops for making "Mr. Crappie" a household name. He was teamed with BPS from 1996 to 2010. Today he has his own line of Wally Marshall Mr. Crappie products. He is a tireless promoter." …Tim Huffman

Wally was born in 1956, is a speaker, promoter, product designer, guided for seven years, won the CAST Classic in 2003. He is a Legends of the Outdoors Hall of Fame member.

Wally says his life changed in 1996 when Bass Pro Shops called as a sponsor. Today Mr. Crappie branding is on Buck Knives, Lew's Rods, Strike King baits and more.

He says his fishing heroes include Don Wallace and Jimmy Houston. Pet peeve: "A gun that won't shoot, a motor that won't start and a woman who won't cook." Biggest crappie, 3.25 in Oklahoma.

How would you like to be remembered? "I hope it's for the Mr. Crappie brand, loving the sport of crappie fishing and being a trailblazer in the industry."

Run & Gun…Todd Huckabee, Travis Bunting & Kyle Schoenherr

"These three fishermen have made an impact on crappie fishing. They have spent many days doing seminars around the country, promoting sponsors and working hard for the sport. Huckabee prefers to guide, Bunting tournament fish and Schoenherr enjoys both. No matter what type crappie fishing they are doing, it's full-speed and serious." …Tim Huffman

Todd Huckabee has his own line of poles and is a workaholic, spending up to 300 days a year on the water or attending shows. He's known as a guide who put customers on a lot of fish. Magazine exposure, especially in late 1990's and 2000's in Crappie World Magazine, along with television and speaking engagements, made him a major player in the crappie-fishing industry. He is a student of crappie and is always searching for answers. Therefore, he provides great in-depth information to those who listen. He is one of the most requested guides in the country.

Travis Bunting is a three-time Classic Champion including the 2017 American Crappie Trail Classic Championship. He and his Dad have many other tournament titles during the past decade and were chosen Sportsman of the Year. Travis has his own line of plastics, Muddy Water Baits. I've been in the boat with him many times doing photo shoots and fishing. Travis uses his electronics to the maximum, spending much of his time finding the right spots before dropping a line into the water. He makes many right decisions during tournament days. Much of his success is due to his partner, father, and expert fisherman, Charles. Together, Travis and Charles make a formidable fishing team.

Huckabee

Bunting

Schoenherr

Kyle Schoenherr has made history in tournament fishing when he and partner Rodney Neuhaus won both the Crappie USA and Crappie Masters Classic in the same year, 2015. More recently they won the 2016 Crappie USA Classic on Kentucky Lake, making them the first team to win back-to-back classics. They have many other impressive titles and awards. Kyle guides in Illinois on three lakes. He has a tremendous work ethic and works hard for fishing clients, media and sponsors. Kyle is carving a special notch in crappie-fishing history.

Closing Comments

I'm sure your list of Difference Makers would have been different than mine. I give a big "Thank You" to the old-timers, many who were not mentioned here, who carved special paths for our sport.

APPENDIX

Special Thanks to Phil & Eva Rambo

Phil and Eva Rambo are friends, good fishermen and people I admire. They have tournament fished for many years, have received well-deserved Sportsmen of the Year awards and have the respect of national tournament fishermen around the country. They still compete despite being up in age, often the oldest fishermen at the tournaments. They have promoted several products for companies, helped the trails they've fished and given seminars at sport shows for many years. They have big hearts and are quick to give a helping hand, kind words and their love of God shows through everything they do.

Phil and Eva kindly proofed this book in the early stages. Since I was slow to publish, the book has since evolved and updated. Thanks to Phil and Eva for your work and early proof. But more importantly for your many years of smiles, sharing stories and being friends on the tournament trail.

Keith "Catfish" Sutton

Keith Sutton is at the top of the Who's-Who list of outdoor media. He is a writer, photographer, editor and lecturer with work in more than 350 publications. He served as editor of Arkansas Wildlife, the publication of the Arkansas Game & Fish Commission, and has twice been named the Conservation Communicator of the Year.

Keith has been a long-time friend and associate in media projects and trips. He is one of the good guys in the business. He provided final proof for this book.

Go to Amazon.com to check out fishing books by Keith Sutton. I promise good reading.

Fishermen Mentioned

Paul Alpers, MO; Dennis Bayles, Jr, AR; Bert Bennett, MO; Charles Bunting, MO; Travis Bunting, MO; Ronnie Capps, TN; Bruce Christian, MO; Steve Coleman, TN; Don Collins, SC; Jim Duckworth, TN; Dan Dannenmueller, AL; Jim Dant, MO; Vic Finkley, MS; Roger Gant, MS; Freddie Gilliland, MO; John Harrison, MS; Sam Heaton, FL; Todd Huckabee, OK; Kevin Jones, MO; Louie Mansfield, MO; Wade Mansfield, MO; Wally Marshall, TX; Garry Mason, TN; Barry Morrow, MO; Loren Nelms, KY; Mike Parrott, NC; Bruno Perotti, MO; Phil Rambo, IN; Barbara Reedy, MO; Jim Reedy, MO; Kyle Schoenherr, IL; Buck Simmons, MS; Rick Solomon, OH; Scott Stafford, MO; Stan Tallant, MS; Darrell Van

Vactor, KY; Mike Walters, OH; Brad Whitehead, AL; Larry Whitely, MO; Brent Work, TN

Manufacturers Mentioned

- Andy's Seasoning (www.andysseasoning.com) Fish breading
- Bandit Lures (www.lurenet.com) 100-, 200- and 300-series crankbaits
- Bass Pro Shops (www.basspro.com) Tourney Special 7-foot medium-heavy poles; Johnny Morris Spinning Reel; Better Breader; Uncle Bucks fish breading; Cottonseed Oil
- Berkley (www.berkley-fishing.com) Flicker Shad crank
- BnM Pole Company (www.bnmpoles.com) 7-foot Sam Heaton; 8-foot Difference; 11-foot Sam Heaton; 14-foot Buck Commander; 16-foot BGJP
- Bobby Garland (www.bobbygarlandcrappie.com) Mo Glo heads, Itty Bit Swim'R; Crappie Rattle
- Bomber (www.bomberlures.com) Fat Free Fingerling; Model 6A
- Charlie Brewer Slider Company (www.sliderfishing.com) Slider jigs
- Drake's (www.drakesbattermix.com) Fish batter mix
- Driftmaster (www.driftmaster.com) Rod racks; Little Duo Holders; Crow's Foot

APPENDIX

- Eagle Claw (www.eagleclaw.com) 214EL hooks
- Lindy Fishing (www.lindyfishingtackle.com) Shadling crankbait; balsa float
- Gamma (www.gammafishing.com) High-vis line
- Garmin (www.garmin.com) Electronics
- Grizzly Jig Company (www.grizzlyjig.com) Google-eye jig; Grizzly jigs
- Huckabee Rods (www.toddhuckabeerods.com) Poles
- Johnson Fishing (www.johnsonfishing.com) Crappie Buster crankbaits
- JR Mad's (www.marionkay.com) Breading & spices
- Midsouth Tackle (www.midsouthtackle.com) Jigs; Super jig; glow jig
- Minn Kota (www.minnkotamotors.com) Terrova
- Mitchell (www.mitchellfishing.com) Spinning reels
- Mr. Crappie (www.mrcrappie.com) High-vis line; 16-foot Trolling poles
- Muddy Water Baits (available at: www.grizzlyjig.com) Jigs
- Off-Shore Tackle (www.offshoretackle.com) Planer boards
- Okuma (www.okumafishing.com) Line-counter reels
- Ozark Rods (www.ozarkrod.com) Poles

- P-Line (www.p-line.com) Line; high-vis line
- Power Poles (www.power-poles.com) Power anchor
- Rapala (www.rapala.com) JSR5 crankbait
- R&D Works (www.cajunfryer.com) Cajun Fryer
- Sure-Life (www.sure-life.com) Crappie Rx; Keep Alive
- Southern Pro Tackle (www.southernpro.com) Tube jig; Umbrella tube; Magnum tube
- Spike-It (www.spikeit.com) Jigs; scent
- Stormr (www.stormrusa.com) Foul-weather gear
- Strike King (strikeking.com) 200 & 300 crankbaits; Sausagehead jig
- Stubby Steve's (www.stubbysteve.com) Attractant scent
- Sufix (www.sufix.com) Line
- TTI Blakemore (www.ttiblakemore.com) Slab Daddy jig; Road Runner Pro Series; Crappie Thunder; Tru-Turn Hooks
- Vicious (www.getvicious.com) High-vis line
- War Eagle Boats (www.wareagleboats.com) Boats
- Yo-Zuri (www.yo-zuri.com) Hybrid line

Jesus Christ, Lord & Savior

Fishing is fun, a great hobby and provides food for the table. I love the thrill of catching and fighting a scrappy crappie, bluegill or other species. But it means little when looking at the big picture of life and death. "If you were to die today, do you know for certain you would go to heaven?" It's not about being good person, or bad person, going to church or not, but it is about a personal relationship with Jesus Christ and trusting Him to save you.

Heaven or hell is your choice by accepting Jesus or not. It isn't difficult. To know Him as your Lord and Savior, visit your local church or talk to a Christian today.

Made in the USA
Monee, IL
09 September 2019